THE
ESSENTIAL
SWEDENBORG

THE ESSENTIAL SWEDENBORG

BASIC RELIGIOUS TEACHINGS
OF EMANUEL SWEDENBORG

Selected and with an introduction by
Sig Synnestvedt

**SWEDENBORG
FOUNDATION**
West Chester, Pennsylvania

First edition, 1970 (Twayne Publishers, Inc.)
First Swedenborg Foundation edition, 1977 (second printing, 1981; third printing, 1984; fourth printing, 1993)
Second Swedenborg Foundation edition, 1995
Third Swedenborg Foundation edition, 2023*

Library of Congress Cataloging-in-Publication Data
Names: Swedenborg, Emanuel, 1688-1772. author. | Synnestvedt, Sig, compiler.
Title: The essential Swedenborg : basic religious teachings of Emanuel Swedenborg / Emanuel Swedenborg ; selected and with an introduction by Sig Synnestvedt.
Description: Third edition. | West Chester, Pennsylvania : Swedenborg Foundation, [2023] | Includes bibliographical references and index. | Summary: "The Essential Swedenborg serves as an introduction to the theology of Swedish scientist-turned-seer Emanuel Swedenborg (1688-1772). This edition provides new translations of selections from Swedenborg's works on some of his key theological topics, including use, charity, life after death, the destiny of humanity, and divine providence"-- Provided by publisher.
Identifiers: LCCN 2022023022 | ISBN 9780877854333 (paperback) | ISBN 9780877857143 (epub)
Subjects: LCSH: New Jerusalem Church--Doctrines. | Theology--Early works to 1800.
Classification: LCC BX8711.A25 2023 | DDC 289/.4--dc23/eng/20220801
LC record available at https://lccn.loc.gov/2022023022

Edited by John Connolly
Design and typesetting by Karen Connor

Printed in the United States of America

* This edition of *The Essential Swedenborg* has been updated, replacing the passages from previous editions with modern translations from the New Century Edition of the Works of Emanuel Swedenborg, as well as with unpublished translations provided by the Swedenborg Foundation.

Swedenborg Foundation
320 North Church Street
West Chester, PA 19380
www.swedenborg.com

Contents

Preface

THE SHEER BULK of Swedenborg's writings has doubtless been a limiting factor in the study of his thought. During his earlier years (1720–45), he wrote on civic, scientific, and philosophical subjects. These contributions fill at least twenty large volumes. During the latter part of his life (1745–72), he turned to theology, and his religious works, not including five volumes of his *Spiritual Diary*, fill thirty additional tomes of more than a quarter million words each. Probably no religious writer has left a larger body of teachings for later generations to study. [1]

During his own lifetime, Swedenborg's contributions were well known in European intellectual circles. Men like Immanuel Kant, Carl Gustaf Tessin, Carl Linnaeus, Hermann Boerhaave, Charles XII of Sweden, Friedrich Christoph Oetinger, Johann Wolfgang von Goethe, Edmund Halley, Christopher Polhem, Jean-Jacques Rousseau, François M. Arouet [Voltaire], and John Wesley knew Swedenborg or his works. Some reacted favorably to his writings; others did not. But few leading intellects of the eighteenth century failed to take note of them.

Swedenborg's fame increased during the nineteenth century. Distinguished thinkers looked on him as one of the great men of all time. Ralph Waldo Emerson, when including Swedenborg in his collection of essays on representative men of history, called him "a colossal soul [who] lies vast abroad on his times, uncomprehended by them, and requires a long focal distance to be seen. . . . One of the missouriums and mastodons of literature, he is not to be measured by whole colleges of ordinary scholars."[2]

Of Swedenborg, Henry James, Sr., wrote, "The incomparable depth and splendour of Swedenborg's genius are shewn in this, that he alone of men has ever dared to bring creation within the bounds of consciousness. . . . He grasped with clear and intellectual vision the seminal principles of things."[3]

Edwin Markham, the American poet who won fame with his "The Man with the Hoe" at the turn of the twentieth century, once said, "There is no doubt that Swedenborg was one of the greatest intellects that has appeared upon the planet." On another occasion, Markham called him "the wisest man in millions. He was the eyeball on the front of the eighteenth century."[4]

Samuel Taylor Coleridge, John Bigelow, Elizabeth Barrett Browning, William Blake, Thomas Carlyle, John Greenleaf Whittier, Edward Everett Hale, Honoré de Balzac, John F. Oberlin, Robert Browning, William Dean Howells, Henri Bergson, James Freeman Clarke, and other nineteenth-century leaders recognized Swedenborg as a man of exceptional insight and mental power.

The twentieth century made scant note of Swedenborg's science or philosophy and paid practically no attention at all to his theology. Yet Swedenborg speaks to modern problems. His teachings deserve more study than they currently receive. "God is dead," say many modern theologians. By this striking phrase, some at least mean that traditional, dogmatic Christianity has died. Swedenborg wrote in a similar vein two hundred and fifty years ago.

His prophecy of a new church that will spread over the world has yet to be realized. But interested persons will find it difficult to avoid the conclusion that his theological writings contain impressive statements that cover the entire range of human existence and are consistent with the clear teachings of the Bible. Helen Keller studied Swedenborg throughout her notable career. She concluded that he was a "Titan Genius" who took "giant strides," served as "an eye among the blind, an ear among the deaf," and emerged eventually as "one of the noblest champions true Christianity has ever known." [5] Thoughtful modern readers may reach similar conclusions after perusing the calm yet intense teachings of this remarkable Swedish philosopher.

This volume contains the basic elements of Swedenborg's thought within the confines of a brief compendium. The task has been attempted before; a score of compendiums of various types have been published. But most of them appeared during the nineteenth century, and nearly all are long out of print. Furthermore, without exception, they have taken forms that appealed primarily to persons already acquainted with Swedenborgian teachings. This study seeks to present the central aspects of Swedenborg's thought to persons who have had little or no previous contact with his writings. Those already initiated into his somewhat difficult terminology, style, and concepts may find this to be a useful overview. Hopefully, those who are new to Swedenborg will be led to consider his works themselves. The Swedish seer deserves a wider audience.

SIG SYNNESTVEDT

Acknowledgments

A BOOK OF this type, which attempts to synthesize the lifetime work of so prolific a writer as Emanuel Swedenborg, can benefit greatly from the pre-publication reactions of talented consultants. I was most fortunate in persuading nine busy persons to give me of their experience in the form of editorial and substantive suggestions. George Dole, E. Bruce Glenn, Bruce Henderson, William R. Kintner, Clayton Priestnal, Donald Rose, Jr., Pelle Rosenquist, Larry Soneson, and Michael Stanley read the manuscript and contributed much to whatever of merit it contains. I want to thank them most warmly for their help while, at the same time, absolving them from any limitations of judgment, errors of syntax, and aberrations of style that are, of course, my own responsibility.

I would also like to thank the members of the Board of Directors of the Swedenborg Foundation for their interest in and support of this project. These thanks go particularly to Tomas Spiers, Executive Secretary, who supplied the original idea of the study, and to Virginia Branston, Manager, and Philip M. Alden, President, all of whom encouraged me throughout the work.

ACKNOWLEDGMENTS

I benefited greatly from the secretarial skills of Elizabeth Clover, who carried the load of typing and proofing endless notes and early drafts, and Diana Wedel, who produced the final version in rapid order in spite of heavy pressure from other responsibilities.

Most especially, I thank my wife Nadine for all her help and patience.

SIG SYNNESTVEDT

Swedenborg Chronology

1688   Born in Stockholm, Sweden, on January 29.

1699–1709 Attended Uppsala University.

1710–15   First journey abroad, to England and elsewhere
             in Europe.

1716   First publications by Swedenborg in the magazine
             Daedalus. Appointed assessor in the Royal College
             of Mines.

1718   Ennoblement of Swedberg family with name changed
             to Swedenborg. Assumption by Swedenborg of seat in
             House of Nobles of Swedish Diet.

1720   Publication of Swedenborg's first book, a philosophic
             work titled *Principles of Chemistry*.

1729–34   Writing and publication of his most important philo-
             sophical works in three volumes, titled *Philosophical
             and Mineralogical Works*.

1735–44   Period of intensive study, writing, and publication on
             the nature of human existence, particularly as regards
             the concept of the soul.

1743–44   First transcendent experiences, visions, or dreams, in
             Holland and England.

1745   "Call" to become a revelator, London, England.

1747   Resignation from the Swedish Board of Mines to allow time for theological writing.

1747–58   Writing and publication of the twelve-volume *Secrets of Heaven,* Swedenborg's first major theological work.

1759–61   Incidents of the Stockholm fire, the Dutch ambassador's receipt, and the Queen's secret, illustrating Swedenborg's clairvoyance.

1769–71   Heresy trial at Gothenburg, Sweden, involving state church accusations against Swedenborg's theology.

1771–72   Publication of the two-volume *True Christianity,* his last major theological work, in Amsterdam, Holland.

1772   Death in London, England, at age 84, on March 29.

THE
ESSENTIAL
SWEDENBORG

Life of Emanuel Swedenborg

*V*ISITORS TO THE cathedral of Uppsala, Sweden, where renowned citizens are interred, may see an impressive red granite sarcophagus on which the name Emanuel Swedenborg appears. The sarcophagus contains the remains of one of Sweden's most accomplished sons. As recently as 1910, when belated recognition was extended to this distinguished intellect, Gustav V, King of Sweden, led in paying him national tribute. Resting in public view has been reserved for kings, archbishops, generals, and prominent intellectuals. Only a score of Swedes have earned this distinction.

Who was Emanuel Swedenborg? What historical position did he hold to warrant such honor and attention? What were his major contributions? The great majority of cathedral visitors will doubtless have no idea of the answer to these questions. The flow of persons through the church will include the educated who may possibly remember Swedenborg's scientific and philosophic contributions to eighteenth-century European thought. A scattered few of Swedenborg's followers will look with awe upon the sarcophagus as the final resting place of the man they consider to have been a new prophet of God on earth.

Ancestors endowed this eminent Swede with multiple talents that determined the course and tenor of his life. On his mother's side, Swedenborg's relatives had long been prominent in the mining industry; his father was a devout clergyman of intelligence and zeal. Into such a household, marked by a harmonious blending of the secular and the sacred, Emanuel was born on the 29th of January, 1688, in the city of Stockholm. Sara Behm, his mother, died when he was eight years old, but her quiet, benevolent spirit molded the character of her third child and second son. Six other children were born to Jesper and Sara Swedberg before her untimely death in 1696.

His father, professor of theology at Uppsala University and dean of the cathedral, later became Bishop of Skara. This post included elevation to the rank of nobleman by Queen Ulrika Eleonora. One result of this honor was the change of the family name from Swedberg to Swedenborg. The bishop also served as chaplain to the royal family and thus had an entrée into the highest social and political circles of Sweden.

From birth, young Swedenborg experienced a family atmosphere characterized by reverence and even religious fervor. The bishop's children, for the most part, were given scriptural names to remind them of their duty to God and the church. Emanuel means "God with us," and Swedenborg's early years suited this theme. The family often discussed religious questions at dinner and other gatherings, and the young boy had opportunities to exchange ideas on faith and life with many clergymen. Years later,

Swedenborg recalled the influence of this early exposure when he wrote, "I was constantly engaged in thought upon God, salvation, and the spiritual diseases ... of men."[6]

But theology, while it bulked large in the Swedberg home, did not eliminate all other subjects of conversation. Politics, war, philosophy, and technology undoubtedly entered the family dialogues. In June of 1699, intellectual stimulation at home led logically to an early enrollment at Uppsala University. Young Emanuel showed high intellectual promise and a catholic outlook.[7] At the time, the university offered four major fields of study: theology, law, medicine, and philosophy. Although Swedenborg majored in the last, his inquiring mind led him into many other fields as well. The faculty of philosophy then included science and mathematics, but he also took courses in law, and since most instruction at Uppsala was still in Latin, he learned this structured language, adding Greek and Hebrew the following year. Subsequent studies and travels enabled Swedenborg to acquire a knowledge of English, Dutch, French, and Italian in addition to his native Swedish and the scriptural languages. For relaxation, he wrote poetry in Latin and studied music. Swedenborg also became suffciently accomplished on the organ, to fill in for the regular accompanist at the church. Versatility and imagination grounded in thoroughness and practicality characterized his academic career.

Upon finishing his formal studies at the university in 1709, he laid plans for an extended period of travel and further study abroad. In 1710, at twenty-two years of age, he went to England for the first time. With the encouragement and financial assistance of his brother-in-law Eric Benzelius, he was able, either under learned individuals or on his own, to study physics, astronomy, and most of the other natural sciences. He also became intensely interested in practical mechanics and learned watchmaking, bookbinding, cabinet work, engraving, and brass instrument construction from skilled English craftsmen. When he went to Holland, he studied the technology of lens grinding, then in its early beginnings. His later studies included cosmology, mathematics, anatomy, physiology, politics, economics, metallurgy, mineralogy, geology, mining engineering, and chemistry. In addition, he became thoroughly versed in the Bible. Moreover, the avid student-scientist made successful efforts to meet recognized leaders in the world of knowledge. In an age when relatively few men became really learned, Swedenborg spent the first thirty-five years of his life in a massive program of formal and self-directed education.

Although he immersed himself in the sciences and other secular pursuits, Swedenborg did not abandon his early religious training. He retained his acceptance of God as the all-pervasive, causal force in the universe. All evidence indicates that he consistently followed the advice that his father gave to him upon leaving Uppsala to accept an appointment in another diocese: "I beg you most earnestly that you fear and love God above all else," the bishop said, "for without this fear of God all other training, all study, all learning is of no account, indeed quite harmful."[8]

In 1716, even before this period of travel and study ended, Swedenborg began a long career in public service. King Charles

XII appointed the talented twenty-eight-year-old scientist to the post of extraordinary assessor in the Royal College of Mines. The position, though partly honorific, also carried varied duties connected with the supervision and development of mining, one of Sweden's most important industries. For thirty-one years, Swedenborg served as a valued member of the Board of Mines. The board met regularly and made decisions affecting all aspects of the mine industry. Swedenborg sometimes received leaves of absence for travel and study, but he attended board meetings faithfully when he was in Sweden.

The post of assessor became far more than a sinecure. Swedenborg's responsibilities included inspecting mines and rendering detailed reports on the quality and amount of mined ore. He spent most of seven different summers traveling around Sweden on these inspection tours, riding horseback or in carriages through miles of forest, staying at local inns, going down in all types of safe and unsafe mines. He was involved in personnel and administrative problems, hiring officials, arbitrating labor disputes, and submitting suggestions for improvements. He even had the unpopular responsibility of collecting national taxes levied on mining. His activities on the Board of Mines finally ended when he resigned in 1747 to give full time to more important tasks to which he believed he had been called.

Swedenborg's public career also included some fifty years of service in the House of Nobles, one of the four estates of the Swedish Riksdag, or legislature. He first took his seat on the ennoblement of his family in 1719. From that time until a few years prior to his death in 1772, Swedenborg attended most of the sessions of the House of Nobles. Deep dedication to the welfare of Sweden led him to make special efforts to plan his travels abroad during times of legislative adjournment. He usually remained in Sweden when the Riksdag was in session, and though not a ready speaker, he repeatedly wrote pamphlets and resolutions on the important questions of the day. On a number of occasions, he expressed views on the nation's economy and tax structure. Foreign policy and matters related to the proper development of Sweden's natural resources also drew his attention.

His most pointed political contest occurred in 1760, during a period of economic stress in Sweden. The councillor of commerce, Anders Nordencrantz, became chairman of a special committee on finance. He was authorized to name all the members of his committee, and their report, not surprisingly, reflected Nordencrantz's thinking on the nation's financial crisis that he had detailed earlier in a lengthy published book. The Nordencrantz analysis contained some useful insights, but his proposals for reform threatened to sweep away the entire structure of the government of Sweden; many felt that his recommendations, if adopted, might tear the fabric of society apart.

Swedenborg, while not unmindful of the need for economic improvement, found Nordencrantz's views generally unacceptable. They put the entire blame for the crisis on government officials. Nordencrantz favored replacing all appointees other than those in church and military positions; these, in turn, would be replaced again every second year thereafter. In brief, Nordencrantz argued for reform by means of a continuous turnover of government officials. The most pernicious feature of his plan would have been vastly increased personal power for the king.

Swedenborg's commentary to the Riksdag objecting to the Nordencrantz report argued that Sweden's problems were caused by a variety of factors in both the private and public sectors rather than simply by the corruption and stupidity of officialdom. He underscored the need for a just balance in criticism of the government in the interest of maintaining an effective structure within which social and civil freedom might gradually be expanded. "Mistakes happen in every country," he wrote, "and with every man—but if a government should be considered simply from its faults, this would be like regarding an individual simply from his failings and deficiencies."[9] In this contest, which he won, Swedenborg showed himself to be a man of moderation who was willing to work toward practical solutions to real problems.

No summary of Swedenborg's public life would be complete without mention of the many occasions on which he put his mechanical genius to work for his country. King Charles XII asked him to serve as his engineering advisor after the king had been impressed by Swedenborg's contributions as editor of the scientific journal *Daedalus,* the first periodical devoted to the natural sciences ever published in Sweden. In the king's service, Swedenborg acted as construction supervisor on several important public works. His assignments involved the creation of a drydock of new design, a canal, machinery for working salt springs, and a system for moving large warships overland. He also showed an inventive imagination in producing feasible sketches of futuristic machines, including an airplane, a submarine, a steam engine, an air gun, and a slow-combustion stove. Although no observer of nature in the 1700s had refined instruments to aid him, leading intellectuals developed the science of the times to a remarkable degree. The limited amount of knowledge made it possible for scholars to be conversant with a broader variety of studies than has been possible since, in the context of the explosion of scientific information during the nineteenth and twentieth centuries. Swedenborg's keen mind coupled with his extensive educational background placed him in the front rank of the learned scientists of the day.

In a century that was ignorant of the existence of oxygen, the circulation of the blood, the composition of water, the makeup of the earth's atmosphere, electricity, spectrum analysis, photography, the concept of the conservation of energy, and the workings of atoms, Swedenborg propounded some impressive theories along with making some incorrect speculations. As his mind developed, he became more interested in generalizing from the findings of others rather than conducting extensive experiments of his own. His thinking exhibited a philosophic rather than an empirical bent.

Nevertheless, in metallurgy and biology, he made experimental discoveries that rank him with the original thinkers of these two disciplines. In metallurgy, his conclusions regarding the proper treatment of iron, copper, and brass advanced both the science and the technology involved.

In biology, his studies of the nervous system and the brain earned him credit for supplying the first accurate understanding of the importance of the cerebral cortex and the respiratory movement of the brain tissues. Modern scholars conclude that Swedenborg's findings pointed the way to "most of the fundamentals of nerve and sensory physiology." [10] He is also praised for his insight into the function and importance of the ductless glands, especially the pituitary. [11]

Had he spent all of his mature years in metallurgy, he might have gone considerably further in these two fields than he did. He refrained from extensive research because he felt that he was not especially gifted in this type of activity. Furthermore, he found that when he did make a modest experimental discovery, he tended to let it draw him away from philosophical generalizations into one-sided explanations too extensively dependent upon his own observation. He believed that there were two main types of mind; on the one hand, there were those gifted in "experimental observation, and endowed with a sharper insight than others, as if they possessed naturally a finer acumen: such are Eustachius, Ruysch, Leeuwenhoek, Lancisi, etc." And then there were others "who enjoy a natural faculty for contemplating facts already discovered, and eliciting their causes. Both are peculiar gifts, and are seldom united in the same person." [12]

Swedenborg had two central philosophic interests: cosmology and the nature of the human soul. From approximately 1720 until 1745, he studied, wrote, and published on these two subjects. His first significant philosophic work, entitled *Chemistry* and published in 1720, emphasized his developing view that everything in nature could be explained mathematically. He rejected the Newtonian concept of permanent, irreducible particles of matter and suggested that everything material was essentially motion arranged in geometric forms.

During the 1720s, he developed his thoughts on the process by which the universe exists and continues. A nearly 600-page manuscript called the *Lesser Principia*, published posthumously, was one product of these efforts, but the great work of his philosophical studies appeared in 1734. It contained three volumes under the general title *Philosophical and Mineralogical Works*. In the first volume, which he called *The Principia*, according to the habit of eighteenth-century philosophers, he presented his primary cosmological conclusions. He based his explanations of the "Principles of Natural Things" on experience, geometry, and reason, and he postulated the creation of a "first natural point" of matter. This first natural point, caused by divine impulse to action, consisted of pure motion. From this point of pure motion, a series of finites descended, each series larger and somewhat less active than the preceding finite. Swedenborg's cosmology thus teems with energy from beginning to end. He argued that activity permeated all three natural kingdoms, animal, vegetable, and mineral. Any material substance emanated energy spheres that interacted with surrounding matter. His studies of magnetism, crystallography, phosphorescence, and metallurgy contributed to his belief in an active universe.

Modern experimentation, particularly in the field of atomic energy, has confirmed many of Swedenborg's cosmological speculations. Svante Arrhenius, noted Nobel Prize chemist and leading figure in the science of physical chemistry, concluded that Buffon, Kant, Laplace, Wright, and Lambert all propounded systems of creation that had been suggested earlier in Swedenborg's *Principia*.[13] The second volume of the *Philosophical and Mineralogical Works* dealt with iron and steel, and the third dealt with copper and brass. In them, not only did Swedenborg treat the technology involved in the use of metals, but he also included further philosophical speculations regarding the makeup and operation of the universe.

Nothing in Swedenborg's *Philosophical and Mineralogical Works* indicated that purely material explanations of the universe satisfied him. His writings rest upon the assumption that divine force underlies all matter, and his speculations next turned to the relationship between the finite and the Infinite. His book-length essay on the Infinite, published in 1734, carried the full title "Outlines of a Philosophical Argument on the Infinite, and the Final Cause of Creation and on the Mechanism of the Operation of Soul and Body." In this and similar studies, Swedenborg judged that although the finite could not know the Infinite, reason compelled humanity to conclude that the human individual was the end of creation. Everything in creation contributed to humanity's functioning as a thinking being. The soul must be the link between God and humanity, the Infinite and the finite, even though humanity could not see or measure that soul.

Swedenborg developed his search for the soul most comprehensively in a study that he called *The Economy of the Animal Kingdom*, published in two lengthy volumes in 1740 and 1741. As the title implies, he found the kingdom of life to be a marvelous unity, tautly structured according to some grand design consistent with the concept of the individual soul as the center of creation. His speculations, which made use of the best anatomical knowledge of the day, focused on the blood as the most likely carrier of the soul. Swedenborg came close to predicting the manner in which the lungs purify the blood, at a time when the discovery of oxygen was fifty years in the future. He then drew upon his earlier studies of the brain and concluded that the operations of the brain and the body, by means of the blood, depended upon a "spirituous fluid" that, while it could not be "known" scientifically, must be the carrier of the soul. He pursued his search for rational explanations of the workings of the soul in a second book, *The Animal Kingdom*, and in other works. He hoped to disperse the "clouds, which darken the sacred temple of the mind" and open a path to faith.[14] Other books from this period, some published and some left in manuscript, include *The Brain, The Senses, The Organs of Generation,* and *Rational Psychology.*

The Economy of the Animal Kingdom drew praise from the scholars of the day. However, reviewers increasingly ignored later works in his search for the soul, and his unpublished manuscripts were, of course, unknown outside the circle of Swedenborg's intellectual intimates.

Swedenborg had gone as far as he could go in attempting to explain the great questions of human existence solely through the faith into which he was born, which was reinforced by his own reasoning powers. The results of his search left him dissatisfied, but a new phase of his life opened, and the remaining years of his career must be viewed in a different perspective.

During 1744 and 1745, he had a number of dreams and visions that moved him profoundly. He sometimes feared and sometimes felt exhilarated by what he experienced. These were years of disquiet that he could not explain satisfactorily, and, typically, he kept silent about them to others, although his *Journal of Dreams* and *Journal of Travel* written during this period recorded his experiences and emotions. He renewed his study of the Bible and began to write a book entitled *Worship and Love of God.*

Then, in April of 1745, he underwent a penetrating experience. In London, while dining alone at an inn where he often went, Swedenborg noted that the room seemed to grow dark. He then saw a vision, and an apparition spoke to him. When the room cleared again, Swedenborg went home to his apartment, considerably stirred by his experience. During that night, he again saw the vision. A spirit reappeared and spoke with him regarding the need for a human person to serve as the means by which God would further reveal himself to humanity in somewhat the manner of the biblical visions of the Old Testament.[15]

Swedenborg came to believe that God had called him to bring a new revelation to the world, and from 1745 until his death twenty-seven years later he spent the bulk of his time adding theological works to his already lengthy scientific and philosophical writings. Few transcendent experiences recorded in human history encompass such a sweeping claim.

He spent the two years immediately following his "call" in further close study of the Bible. He wrote some 3,000 folio pages of unpublished commentary and prepared an extended *Bible Index* that he used in all of his further works on theology. He perfected his knowledge of Hebrew and Greek in order to study the Bible in the original texts and, in effect, made a new translation of many of the books of both the Old and New Testaments. In 1747, he began publication of his most extended theological work, *Secrets of Heaven*. This study of the books of Genesis and Exodus runs to more than 7,000 pages, or about three million words. The subtitle of this multi-volume work asserted that the "secrets of heaven" it contained are "in Sacred Scripture, or the Word of the Lord" and were presented along with "Amazing Things Seen in the World of Spirits and in the Heaven of Angels."

Theological writings continued to flow from Swedenborg's pen. He wrote eight volumes explaining the Book of Revelation and single volumes entitled *Divine Providence, Divine Love and Wisdom,* and *The Four Doctrines* (i.e., *The Lord, Sacred Scripture, Life,* and *Faith*). He presented an account of experiences in the other world in the highly descriptive volume titled *Heaven and Hell.* In 1768, he published a long volume on the subject of marriage under the title *Marriage Love (Conjugial Love).* Shorter works dealt with a variety of subjects.[16]

There are several aspects of the theological phase of Swedenborg's career. First, for much of the period, he wrote and published anonymously, and therefore few, even among his close friends, knew the nature of the theological studies as they evolved. Second, he invested a considerable amount of his own funds in the process since none of his theological studies enjoyed any significant circulation. He gave away many copies anonymously, to clergymen, universities, and libraries. Third, he lived a normal though sometimes secluded life during the early theological years. Unmarried, he was much alone with his books, often in a small summerhouse that he built at the back of the garden of his Stockholm property. Fourth, experiences in his last years reversed the anonymous and secluded pattern of his life as his works became widely diffused in learned circles. Finally, he remained convinced that the Lord had commissioned him to bring a new revelation to humanity. Fulfillment of this commission depended upon a dual existence in both the spiritual and natural worlds alternately, for year upon year as his commentaries multiplied.

Swedenborg made no effort to establish a religious sect or to induce people to form themselves into a church following. In fact, his efforts to remain anonymous with regard to his theological works lasted until 1759. In that year, an incident occurred in Sweden that brought him considerable notoriety and that eventually led many to connect Swedenborg for the first time with his unusual theological works, particularly *Heaven and Hell*. In July, in the city of Gothenburg, approximately 300 miles from Stockholm, while he dined with friends at the home of William Castel, a wealthy local merchant, Swedenborg became pale and disturbed, withdrew for a time to the garden, and returned with news that a great fire had broken out in Stockholm not far from his home. He said that the fire was spreading rapidly and he feared that some of his manuscripts would be destroyed. Finally, at 8:00 P.M., he spoke with relief: "Thank God! The fire is extinguished the third door from my house!"

Persons present, disturbed by the incident since some had homes or friends in Stockholm, were impressed by Swedenborg's apparent clairvoyance. The same evening one of them told the story to the provincial governor, and he, in turn, requested that Swedenborg render him a full account. The next day, Sunday, Swedenborg gave the governor details regarding the nature and extent of the fire and the means by which it had been extinguished. News of the alleged fire spread widely in the city of Gothenburg, and the subject became the general topic of conversation.

Not until Monday evening did a messenger arrive, from the Stockholm Board of Trade, with details on the fire.[17] Since they agreed with those Swedenborg had given, the general curiosity aroused made him a public figure, and not long afterward his authorship of *Heaven and Hell* and *Secrets of Heaven* became known. A variety of prominent persons, curious to meet with a man who claimed to be able to see into the spiritual world, began to write accounts of Swedenborg and his habits. Those who had not yet had an opportunity to meet him tended to conclude that Swedenborg had become insane. After meeting and talking with him, they found him, on the contrary, to be quite reasonable. They frequently ended in a quandary, not willing to accept his sweeping claims, yet convinced of his sanity.

In the spring of the following year, another incident occurred that further revealed Swedenborg's strange powers. The widow of the Dutch ambassador in Stockholm, Mme. de Marteville, became interested in Swedenborg's alleged power to converse with spirits. She hoped that he might be able to help her in a practical matter. A silversmith had presented her with a large bill for a silver service that her husband had purchased before his death. She felt sure that her husband had paid the bill, but she could find no receipt. Swedenborg agreed to ask her husband about it if he saw him in the spiritual world. A few days later, Swedenborg reported that he had seen her husband and that the ambassador had told him that he would tell his wife where the receipt was hidden. Eight days later, Mme. de Marteville dreamed her husband told her to look behind a particular drawer in the desk. She did so and found not only the receipt but also a diamond hairpin that had been missing. The next morning, Swedenborg called on the widow, and, before she told him of her dream and discovery, he reported that he had again conversed with her husband the preceding night and that the ambassador had left the conversation to tell his wife of the missing receipt.

An even more striking incident concerned the "Queen's secret." In the fall of 1761, Count Ulric Scheffer invited Swedenborg to go to the court with him to visit Queen Lovisa Ulrika, who had become interested in Swedenborg through hearing of his varied abilities. The queen asked if he would communicate with her late brother, Augustus William, who had died two years before. Swedenborg agreed to do so and a few days later called at the royal residence, presented the queen with copies of some of his books, and then in a private audience at the far end of the room told her some secret that caused her to show great amazement. She exclaimed that only her brother could have known what Swedenborg told her. The incident became widely known and discussed in Swedish social circles.

These three examples of Swedenborg's clairvoyant abilities, along with lesser incidents, served to spread his fame. He continued to live and write as before, but curious persons often interrupted his studies; many sought to visit with the man who claimed, in a calm and reasonable way, to be able to converse with angels.

The great German philosopher Immanuel Kant's reaction to Swedenborg's visionary powers is of interest in this connection. Although Kant never met Swedenborg himself, he wrote to him and also sent personal messages through mutual friends. Kant, the great rationalist, tended to discount all stories of mystical experience, but the persistent and authoritative reports on Swedenborg's powers gave him repeated pause. At times, he wrote favorably; at times, quite the reverse. However, Kant's continuing interest is indicated by a variety of evidence. Even his most critical survey, *Dreams of a Spirit-Seer,* published in 1766, in which Kant attempted to denigrate Swedenborg, reveals doubts regarding the basis for his own ridicule. In short, Kant must be numbered among those intellects of Swedenborg's day who experienced diffculty explaining satisfactorily the theological phase of Swedenborg's distinguished career.

During Swedenborg's final years, a variety of old friends and new acquaintances wrote accounts of their impressions of him.

His claims seemed preposterous to many, yet few who met and talked with him had anything really adverse to say of him. They were perplexed at his accounts of conversations with spirits but found him otherwise to be a gentle, humorous man with a relaxed, benign air. Occasionally, when callers tried to make fun of him, Swedenborg spoke cuttingly, but in general he was the perfect host.

In 1768, Swedenborg, eighty years of age but in excellent health and spirits, set out on the next-to-last extensive journey of his life on earth. Many previous trips had taken him all over Europe, including Italy, France, Germany, Holland, and England. On this occasion, he went first to France and then to England, where he took lodgings with a young couple in Wellclose Square, London. During the summer, he spent many hours working on his last great theological work, a two-volume study entitled *True Christianity*. He also enjoyed walking in the nearby parks, talking with acquaintances, and visiting friends. One associate said of him during this period, "Some one might think that Assessor Swedenborg was eccentric and whimsical; but the very reverse was the case. He was very easy and pleasant in company, talked on every subject that came up, accommodating himself to the ideas of the company; and he never spoke on his own views, unless he was asked about them." [18]

In 1769, he returned to Sweden, partly to answer charges of heresy that had been leveled against him by some of the prelates of the Lutheran state church. He had been informed by friendly correspondents that his theological writings were the cause of much controversy in the Lutheran Consistory in Gothenburg. By this time, several of Swedenborg's works had been translated into Swedish, and followers, among both the clergy and the laity, spoke out in favor of his theology.

In September of 1768, a country parson precipitated a decisive debate by introducing a resolution in the Gothenburg Consistory calling for measures to stop the circulation of works at variance with the dogmas of Lutheranism. The parson objected particularly to Swedenborg's writings. While some members of the Consistory insisted that no judgment be rendered until all members had thoroughly studied the works in question, Dean Ekebom, the ranking prelate, announced that he found Swedenborg's doctrines to be "corrupting, heretical, injurious, and in the highest degree objectionable." Although he confessed that he had not read any works other than *Revelation Unveiled* (*Apocalypse Revealed*) with any care, he concluded that Swedenborg's views on the nature of the Divine, the Bible, the Holy Supper, faith, and other basic teachings should be suppressed as dangerous to established religious concepts. He charged Swedenborg with Socinianism, or refusal to accept the divinity of Christ.

On being apprised of these charges, Swedenborg wrote vigorously in his own defense. The Socinianism charge particularly upset him, and he wrote, "I look upon the word Socinian as a downright insult and diabolical mockery." One of Swedenborg's most carefully argued lines of theological reasoning directly refutes Socinianism and argues for the acceptance of Christ as God on earth.

The dispute became inflamed and shifted to the political level when the matter was brought up in the national Diet. The dean's legal advisor and chief prosecutor urged that "the most energetic measures" be taken to "stifle, punish, and utterly eradicate Swedenborgian innovation and downright heresies by which we are encompassed ... so that the boar which devastates and the wild beast which desolates our country may be driven out with a mighty hand." The Royal Council, appointed through the Diet, finally rendered its report in April 1770. The anti-Swedenborgians won most of what they were seeking. Swedenborg's clerical supporters were ordered to cease using his teachings, and customs officials were directed to impound his books and stop their circulation in any district unless the nearest consistory granted permission. In its own words, the Royal Council "totally condemned, rejected, and forbade the theological doctrines contained in Swedenborg's writings."

While the dispute dragged on for three more years, Swedenborg continued to protest the decision of the council and petitioned the king himself. The Royal Council referred the matter to the Götha Court of Appeals, which asked several universities, including Swedenborg's alma mater, Uppsala, to make a thorough study of Swedenborg's ideas. The universities, however, asked to be excused. Their theological faculties found nothing that they felt they should condemn, but, on the other hand, they had no inclination to put bishops and entire consistories on trial for false accusation, the only means by which the anti-Swedenborgian decisions could be reversed. The matter quieted down. Some clergymen preached Swedenborgian ideas; most did not. Swedenborg continued to write and speak as he pleased in his few remaining years on earth.[19]

Completion of the crowning work of his theological period engrossed him. Although eighty-two years of age, he undertook his final, eleventh, foreign journey to promote this effort. Apparently, he felt he would not return to Sweden, for he made farewell calls on the members of the Board of Mines, on supporters, and on close friends. He arranged a pension for his faithful housekeeper, made lists of his possessions for estate distribution, and told his long-time friend and neighbor, Carl Robsahm, "Whether I shall come again, that . . . I do not yet know; but of this I can assure you, for the Lord has promised to me, that I shall not die, until I shall have received from the press this work . . . , which is now ready to be printed."[20] He referred to the manuscript to be published in 1771 in Holland under the title *Vera Christiana Religio* (*True Christianity*).

A skeptical but generally friendly observer visited Swedenborg in Amsterdam during the printing of *True Christianity* and reported that the seer, in spite of his advanced age, worked "indefatigably" and even "in an astonishing and superhuman way," reading proofs and returning them to the publisher. He found Swedenborg convinced that he served, as the title page stated, in the capacity of "The Servant of the Lord Jesus Christ."[21]

When the book was printed, Swedenborg left Amsterdam and crossed the Channel to England. He arrived in London in early September of 1771 and again rented quarters with a family named Shearsmith in Great Bath Street. Although his health declined, he continued to work at his books. But in December, he suffered a stroke that destroyed his ability to speak and rendered him unconscious for most of three weeks. During January and February, he gradually recovered and again talked with visitors.

He wrote to John Wesley, the noted English minister, and told him that he would be happy to discuss religion with him if Wesley could come to London. Swedenborg mentioned that he had learned in the world of spirits that Wesley wanted to talk with him about theology. Wesley expressed his great surprise to friends regarding Swedenborg's invitation because he did not recall having told anyone of his interest in the Swedish seer. Wesley answered Swedenborg's letter with hopes that he would be welcomed upon completion of a six months' journey on which he had just embarked. When he received Wesley's reply, Swedenborg remarked that six months would be too long since he, Swedenborg, would permanently enter the world of spirits on the 29th of March, 1772. The maid who attended Baron Swedenborg during his final months also reported that he predicted the exact date of his death.[22]

Several friends visited Swedenborg during March and urged him to make a final statement regarding the truth or falsity of the new revelation that had been flowing from his pen for so many years. Swedenborg answered pointedly: "I have written ... nothing but the truth, as you will have it more and more confirmed hereafter all the days of your life, provided you always keep close to the Lord, and faithfully serve Him alone, in shunning evils of all kinds as sins against Him, and diligently searching His Sacred Word, which from beginning to end bears incontestable testimony to the truth of the doctrines I have delivered to the world." On another occasion, in answer to a similar question, Swedenborg said, "As true as you see me before your eyes, so true is everything that I have written; and I could have said more, had it been permitted. When you enter eternity, you will see every thing, and then you and I shall have much to talk about." [23]

On Sunday, March 29, 1772, Mrs. Shearsmith and Elizabeth Reynolds, the maid, observed Swedenborg waking from a long sleep. He asked the women to tell him the time of day. They replied that it was five o'clock. "Dat be good," Swedenborg said. "Me tank you, God bless you." He then "heaved a gentle sigh, and expired in the most tranquil manner." [24]

Shortly after Swedenborg's death, an energetic Londoner named Robert Hindmarsh came upon a copy of *Heaven and Hell*. Upon reading it he became a convert and organized the first group of followers of Swedenborg. Meeting regularly in London, the Hindmarsh circle began to expound the tenets of Swedenborgian theology. Swedish followers organized under the leadership of Johan Rosén and Gabriel A. Beyer, two noted intellectuals who had been reading Swedenborg for some time. James Glen, a sometime-member of the Hindmarsh group in England, brought copies of Swedenborg's writings to Philadelphia in 1784, and Swedenborgianism in America dates from Glen's efforts to establish Swedenborgian reading circles in the Quaker city and elsewhere. Although the total number of Swedenborg followers has never grown large, there are active adherent groups all over the world.

Swedenborg's teachings exert a clear and direct influence on those who regard themselves as followers of the new faith. Swedenborgians study his theological writings, and, like members of other religious sects, they attempt to put the principles expressed into effect in their own lives. The less tangible evidence of Swedenborg's influence—his effect on the mainstream of world thought—remains to be evaluated. Scholars who attempt the task may conclude, with Arthur Conan Doyle, that they have a "mountain peak of mentality" under scrutiny.[25]

Part One

THE NATURE OF LIFE

S
WEDENBORG'S WRITINGS COVER a wide range of subjects. The great philosophic questions that have attracted
all of the powerful minds of history ("What is the nature
of the universe?" "Of God?" "Of humanity?" "What is the destiny
of each?" "How may these things be known?" "What is morality?"
"What constitutes the good life?") receive attention in Swedenborg's teachings. From earliest youth to old age, individuals continuously make choices that affect both their own lives and the
lives of those around them. Some of these choices involve minute, personal questions that make little difference to anyone but
the person making the judgment. Most of these everyday choices,
however, have a larger scope. The courses of human lives proceed
in a common sea, and the route that an individual takes as well
as the wake she or he leaves affects others. "No man is an island,"
wrote the poet; Swedenborg agrees. Further, he teaches that a
person's relationship with their fellow human beings determines

their relationship with their God. Part I of this study, "The Nature of Life," deals primarily with questions concerning men and women, while Part II, "The Source of Life," treats of more abstruse matters regarding the divine hand behind human affairs. Together the two parts of this compendium present the essence of the Swedenborgian view of life.

Certain assumptions underlie all of Swedenborg's teachings, concrete and abstract alike. In sum, Swedenborg presumes a divine center of the universe from which flow all creative forces that find expression in both a spiritual and a natural kingdom of consciousness. Love and wisdom, united in use, constitute the personal God he pictures. The human individual is the highest end of creation. Human happiness to eternity in heaven is the ultimate object of all divine action.

Humanity, while it has no life from itself, has been created to feel that it controls its own destiny. And indeed, according to Swedenborg, human beings do control their own destiny in that they may choose a life that conforms to divine order—one of charity and use—or one that does not. Freedom to accept or reject God sets the stage for the human drama. The quality of a human being's life determines her or his place in the spiritual world after death.

God, according to Swedenborg, has always provided communication with humanity both by direct revelation and through the workings of nature, although humanity has not always listened to divine teaching. When human beings act in accord with the divine plan, their life is blessed ultimately if not at once;

when they do not so act, they separate themselves from the divine order. But happiness, in Swedenborg's view, is entirely within a person's grasp if she or he only will listen, reason, and apply themselves to a good life. By these means, human beings can direct their energies toward a life of useful service to others and eventually enter heaven.

FREEDOM

Human beings live in a world in which freedom and rationality balance each other and produce order. The twin essentials of freedom in order form the crucible of life. Neither can be slighted without harm to human development. Swedenborgian thought rests upon a firm and explicit belief in the freedom of the human will.

As long as we are in this world we are in between hell and heaven—hell is below us and heaven above us—and during this time we are kept in a freedom to turn toward hell or toward heaven. If we turn toward hell we are turning away from heaven, while if we turn toward heaven we are turning away from hell. (*Life* §19)[26]

Our free choice comes from our sense that we have life within us as if it were our own. God allows us to feel this way for the sake of our partnership [with him]. A partnership with God would not be possible if it were not reciprocal, and it becomes reciprocal when we act freely, and completely as if we were on our own. If we were not allowed by God to feel this way, we would not be human and our life would not be eternal. Our reciprocal partnership with God is what makes us humans and not animals and enables us to live to eternity after death. What makes all this possible is our free choice in spiritual matters. (*True Christianity* §504)

Since no one can reform except in freedom, our freedom is never taken from us, however much it may seem to be. It is an eternal law that each of us is free on deeper levels . . . in order that a desire for goodness and truth can be instilled in us. (*Secrets of Heaven* §2876)

It seems to people . . . that their life is . . . their own . . . because of freedom. Freedom is the ability to think, want, say, and do things of your own accord, or as if of your own accord. . . . This is why people are given freedom as one with their life. . . . If [this freedom] were in any way . . . taken away or diminished, to the same degree a person would not sense or feel like it was really them living. . . . And to that same degree all the joy of their life would be taken away and diminished, and they would become a slave. (*Revelation Explained* §1138)

No one can see what enslavement and freedom are without seeing the source of each. And no one can see the source except from the Word.[27] In addition, no one can see the source without seeing how matters stand with human beings in regard to the desires that occupy their will and the thoughts that fill their intellect. This is how matters stand with humans in regard to their feelings and their thoughts: No one, no matter who—human, spirit, or angel—can will and think on her or his own but only from others; and these others cannot will or think on their own but must all do so from yet others; and so on. So everyone wills

and thinks from the original source of life, who is the Lord. . . .
Evil and falsity connect with the hells. . . . Goodness and truth,
however, connect with heaven. (*Secrets of Heaven* §§2885–86)

Few know what freedom and lack of freedom are. Everything that springs from love and its pleasure seems free, while
everything that opposes it seems nonfree. Anything that springs
from love for ourselves and worldly advantages and from the
cravings they excite seems free to us; but the freedom is hellish.
On the other hand, anything that springs from love for the Lord
and love for our neighbor and therefore from a love for what is
good and true is freedom itself—the freedom of heaven. (*Secrets
of Heaven* §2870)

We always long to move from nonliberty to liberty, because
this is central to our life. Obviously, then, what does not come of
freedom, of voluntary choice or willingness, is in no way pleasing
to the Lord. When we worship the Lord in nonfreedom, we worship him with nothing of our own. It is our outer shell that acts,
or rather is forced to act. (*Secrets of Heaven* §1947)

Some people live good lives and believe that the Lord governs the universe; that he alone is the source of all the good that
comes of love and charity and all the truth that leads to faith;
[and] that life itself comes from him. . . . The condition of these
people is such that they can receive the gift of heavenly freedom,
and peace too, because under these circumstances they trust only
in the Lord and do not let anything else bother them. They are
certain that under his care, everything leads forever toward what
is good, blessed, and happy for them. People who believe they

control their own lives, though, constantly feel troubled. They constantly become embroiled in their appetites, in worries about the future, and so in many forms of anxiety. Because of their belief, evil cravings and distorted convictions also cling to them. (*Secrets of Heaven* §2892)

Within human freedom, there are two things that come from the Lord's presence and desire to connect with us. One of the two is that we have the ability and opportunity to think positively about the Lord and about our neighbor. . . . If we think positively, the door is opened. If we think negatively, the door is closed. Thinking positively about the Lord and about our neighbor does not come from the person and their ego. Instead it comes from the Lord, who is always present and who, through his ongoing presence, gives us that opportunity and ability. However, thinking negatively about the Lord and about our neighbor comes from ourself and from our ego. Another result of the freedom we have from the Lord's continual presence with us is that we can refrain from evil. To the degree that we refrain, the Lord opens the door and comes in. However, the Lord is not able to come in as long as there are evils in our thoughts and desires, because they stand in the way. . . . The Lord also gives us the ability to understand the evils that occur in our thoughts and desires, along with the ability to understand the truths that shatter them. This is because we have the Word, where those truths are uncovered. (*Revelation Explained* §248)

All of us have earthly freedom by heredity. It is what makes us love nothing but ourselves and the world. . . . Rational freedom comes from a love for our own reputation, either for the sake of respect or for the sake of profit. This love finds its pleasure in putting on the outward appearance of moral character. . . . Spiritual freedom comes from a love for eternal life. The only people who arrive at this love and its pleasure are people who think that evils are sins and therefore do not want to do them, and who at the same time turn toward the Lord. (*Divine Providence* §73)

We have been granted free choice in spiritual matters from the womb even to our last moment in this world, and afterward to eternity. (*True Christianity* §499)

ORDER

To Swedenborg, human freedom constitutes the central ingredient of individuality. But he adds that without order, nothing, human beings included, could be free. Freedom and order are so interrelated that one cannot fully exist without the other. The universe was created in perfect order, but humanity has freedom to create disorder.

The Lord is order itself, so where he is present, there is order, and where there is order, he is present. (*Secrets of Heaven* §5703)

God is the divine design because he is substance itself and form itself. He is substance because from him come all things that subsist, that came into existence in the past, and that are coming into existence now. He is form because every quality of [these] substances arose and arises from him. Quality comes from no other source than form. . . . From himself God imposed a design on the universe and on every single thing in it. (*True Christianity* §53)

Human beings were created as forms of the divine design. We have been created as forms of the divine design because we have been created as images and likenesses of God, and since God is the design itself, we have therefore been created as images and likenesses of that design. The divine design originally took shape, and it continues to exist, from two sources: divine love and divine wisdom. We human beings have been created as vessels for these two things. Therefore the design that divine love and wisdom follow in acting upon the universe . . . has been built into us. . . . Heaven in its entirety is a form of the divine design in its largest possible manifestation. In the sight of God, heaven is like one human being. (*True Christianity* §65)

The facts about the life force in everyone—human, spirit, and angel—are that it flows in from the Lord alone (who is life itself) and . . . pours into every individual, in a pattern and sequence that are beyond comprehension. The life that flows in, however, is received by each of us according to our disposition. Good people receive goodness and truth as goodness and truth, but evil people receive goodness and truth as evil and falsity, and these even turn into evil and falsity in them. The situation here resembles that of sunlight. The sun pours into every object on earth, but each receives it in accord with its nature. The light takes on beautiful colors in beautiful forms, and ugly colors in ugly forms. (*Secrets of Heaven* §2888)

The proper pattern is for us to accept goodness and truth as they issue from the Lord. When we do, everything we intend and think is orderly. Suppose, though, that we do not accept goodness and truth according to the code set by the Lord; suppose we believe instead that everything is blind ebb and flow . . . [or that] it is the result of our own prudence. In that case we pervert the proper order. We take what has been ordained and we appropriate it to ourselves, seeking only our own welfare, not our neighbor's, unless our neighbor curries our favor. (*Secrets of Heaven* §6692)

There are laws of the divine design imposed on human beings that indicate that we are to acquire truths from the Word for ourselves and that we are to base our thinking on them in an earthly way and, as much as we can, in a rational way. This is how we develop an earthly faith for ourselves. On God's side, there are laws of the divine design dictating that he is to come closer, fill those truths with his own divine light, take our earthly faith . . . , and fill it with a divine essence. (*True Christianity* §73)

People who do not understand divine omnipotence are able to reckon either that no divine design exists, or that God can act just as easily against his design as with it. But in fact, without the divine design no creation would have been possible. The first element of the divine design is that we are an image of God, so that we can be perfected in love and wisdom and therefore become more and more of an image [of him]. God continually works toward this within us. . . . Therefore it is the same whether you say "to act against the divine design" or "to act against God." God could not act against his own divine design, since that would in fact be acting against himself. Therefore he leads every human being in a manner in keeping with his being that design. The wandering and the fallen he leads into that design; the resistant he leads toward it. If it would have been possible to create the human race without endowing it with free choice in spiritual matters, what then would have been easier for the omnipotent God than to induce everyone on the whole planet to believe in the Lord? Could he not have installed this faith in everyone, either directly or indirectly? He could have done so directly through his own absolute power and his constant, irresistible efforts to save us; or he could have done it indirectly through inflicting torment upon our consciences and devastating convulsions upon our bodies, and threatening us with death if we did not accept. He could have achieved the same result by opening hell to us and surrounding us with devils holding terrifying torches in their hands, or by calling up from hell dead people we once knew who now look like horrible specters. (*True Christianity* §500)

The Lord never does anything contrary to his design because he himself is the design. The divine truth that emanates from him is what establishes the design, and divine truths are the laws of the design by which the Lord is leading us. Saving people by unmediated mercy is contrary to the divine design, and anything contrary to the divine design is contrary to the divine nature. The divine design is heaven for us. We have distorted it by living contrary to its laws, which are divine truths. The Lord brings us back into the design out of pure mercy, through the laws of the design; and to the extent that we are brought back, we accept heaven into ourselves. This shows . . . that the Lord's divine mercy is pure mercy but not unmediated. (*Heaven and Hell* §523)

To welcome [the Lord's] orderly pattern into ourselves is to be saved, which is accomplished only by living in accord with the Lord's commandments. (*Secrets of Heaven* §10659)

That people who do not live by the commandments and laws that make up the divine plan do not live in the Lord, so their sight of the Deity becomes dim. When I speak of living by the divine plan . . . I mean being led by the Lord by means of goodness. (*Secrets of Heaven* §8512)

Animals are in the proper pattern of their life and cannot destroy what is within them from the spiritual world because they are not rational. It is different for us, who think from the spiritual world. Because we have corrupted ourselves by living contrary to the design that reason itself has recommended to us, we cannot escape being born into total ignorance, so that we can be led from there, by divine means, back into the pattern of heaven. (*Heaven and Hell* §108)

If we followed the code we were created to live by, we would possess love for our neighbor and love for the Lord, these being the loves proper to us. Under those circumstances, we would excel all animals by being born not just into all knowledge but even into all spiritual truth and heavenly goodness. So we would be born into all wisdom and understanding. (*Secrets of Heaven* §6323)

Everything that comes from the Deity, you see, begins with him and progresses in order to its stopping point, which means that it progresses through the heavens into the world. There, on its final plane, it comes to rest. (*Secrets of Heaven* §10634)

The proper order is for the heavenly dimension to act on the spiritual dimension and adapt it to its own purposes. The spiritual dimension should act on the rational and adapt this to its own purposes. And the rational dimension should act on the factual and adapt this to its own purposes. This is indeed the pattern that we follow in childhood, when we are learning, but the appearance is exactly the opposite: we seem to proceed from facts to rational thinking, from this to spiritual ideas, and finally to heavenly concepts. This is the way it appears because this is how a path to the heavenly plane—the deepest plane—opens up. All instruction is simply an opening of the path. (*Secrets of Heaven* §1495)

The Lord is in equal control of what comes last and what comes first in us. . . . The overall design comes from the Lord and follows a progression from first to last. This design contains nothing that is not divine, and as a result the Lord is necessarily as fully present in what is last as in what is first. The one follows from the other in keeping with the design's course of progress. (*Secrets of Heaven* §6473)

USE

Probably Swedenborg's concept of use permeates his view of life more completely than does any other single idea. Down through the centuries, philosophers and theologians have discussed the ingredients of the "good life." Swedenborg joins this discussion with an abundance of detail and illustration. Use, by which Swedenborg means "the service of others," unifies all of creation. Both worlds—spiritual and natural—

rest upon this concept of use. Human beings enjoy true happiness when they reach out to serve others, while at the same time fulfilling their particular destiny in turning their individual talents to the pursuit of excellence in fields consistent with their loves. Use, to Swedenborg, means "good."

We are born for no purpose but to be useful to the community we live in and to our neighbor as long as we are alive in the world, and to serve at the Lord's good pleasure in the other world. The situation resembles that in the human body. Every part of our anatomy has to serve a function, including elements that in themselves are worthless—fluids that exist to be excreted, for instance, as the many types of saliva do, and the different types of bile, and others. Not only do they have to work on the food, they also have to extract waste products and clean out the intestines. (*Secrets of Heaven* §1103)

We do not live unless at the same time we live for others. This is the basis of community, which otherwise would not exist. Living for others means being of service. Acts of service are what tie a community together. . . . There is an infinite number of such acts. There are spiritual acts that flow from our love for God and love for our neighbor; there are moral and civic acts that come from a love for the community and the state in which we live and from love for the colleagues and fellow citizens with whom we live; there are earthly acts of service that flow from our love for the world and from its demands; and there are physical acts that flow from our need to take care of ourselves for the sake of those higher forms of service. All these forms of service have been inscribed on humanity in the order of their importance and follow in a series one after the other. (*Marriage Love* §18)

Whatever we know, whatever we understand or have wisdom in, and whatever we accordingly intend need to have usefulness as their end in view. . . . What leads to usefulness is knowing what is good and true, and usefulness itself is to will and do what is good and true. (*Secrets of Heaven* §5293)

The Lord leads us through the desire for usefulness. (*Draft of "Supplements"* §170)

Since desires are the determining factor within every useful action, and the useful action is subject to the desire, it makes sense that there are as many types of desire as there are types of useful action. (*Draft on Divine Love* §9)

We . . . are what our use is. However, there are numerous different kinds of uses. Generally, they are either heavenly or hellish. Heavenly uses are those that serve the church, the country, society, and other people, whether they are greater or smaller, serving either directly or indirectly, for the sake of those groups. Hellish uses, on the other hand, are those that serve only ourselves and our own goals. In this case, we ourselves are the priority, and not the church, the country, society, or other people. We all should take care of ourselves, and provide what we need and what our lives require, but out of real love, not self-centered love. When the love of being useful is our top priority and our love for ourselves and for worldly things is secondary, then being useful is our spiritual goal, and the other things are our earthly goals. In this case, what is spiritual is in charge, and what is worldly serves it. (*Revelation Explained* §1193)

Being useful consists in doing our work and meeting our obligations well, faithfully, honestly, and fairly. People have only the vaguest notion of what charitable deeds really mean in the Word (which are also called "works" or even "fruit"). Because of the literal sense of the Word, people think it means giving to the poor, helping people in need, donating to widows and orphans, and the like. This type of usefulness, though, is not what "fruit" and "works" refer to. Instead, they refer to faithfully, honestly, and fairly doing our work, meeting our obligations, and conducting our business. They refer to taking into consideration the common good—the well-being of the public—as well as the good of the country and its communities large and small, and our fellow citizens, friends, and relatives, all of whom . . . are our neighbor from the broadest to the narrowest sense. Whoever does this, whether they are a priest, a leader, a military officer, a business person, or a laborer, performs useful functions on a daily basis. A priest does it through preaching, leaders and officers through administration, a business person through their trade, and a laborer through their work. For example, judges who make decisions faithfully, honestly, fairly, and well do something useful for their neighbor every time they hand down a judgment. Likewise, ministers whenever they teach, and so on. (*Draft on Divine Wisdom* §11)

"Pursuit" and "occupation" mean any focus on service. When people are committed to some pursuit or occupation—that is, to some service—then their minds have boundaries and a perimeter, as though they were enclosed by a circle within which they gradually develop into a truly human form. (*Marriage Love* §249)

Useful things include not only the necessities of life—food, clothing, and shelter for oneself and one's own—but also the good of the country, community, and fellow citizen. Business is useful when it is the real love and money is a subservient, supporting love, provided the merchant avoids and recoils from fraud and deceptive practices as sins. It is different when money is the real love and business is the subservient, supporting love. This is greed, the root of evils. (*Divine Providence* §220)

Since actions need to be uses, they are more or less good depending on the importance of use they serve. The best actions are ones that are taken to forward the usefulness of the church. The next best are the ones taken to forward the usefulness of the country, and so on. The goodness of the act is determined by the use it serves. (*Revelation Explained* §975)

Both eminence and the rank it offers are physical and time-bound when we focus on ourselves and our role in them and not on the state and service. Then we . . . think to ourselves that the state exists for our sake and not that we exist for the sake of the state. It is like monarchs who think that the realm and all its citizens exist for their sake and not that they are monarchs for the sake of the realm and its citizens. The very same eminence and rank are spiritual and eternal, though, when we see ourselves and our role as existing for the sake of the state and service, and not the state and service for our own sake. (*Divine Providence* §220)

The Lord's kingdom is a kingdom of purposes that are functions or—which amounts to the same thing—of functions that are purposes. For this reason, the universe has been so created and formed by the Divine that functions can . . . present themselves in act or in results, first in heaven and then in this world, and so step by step all the way to the lowest things in nature. . . . In the three kingdoms of earthly nature, all the things that happen according to the design are [outward] forms of their functions or results formed by function for function. . . . As for us, though, our acts are services in forms to the extent that we live according to the divine design—that is, in love for the Lord and in thoughtfulness toward our neighbor. To that extent, our acts are correspondences that unite us to heaven. In general terms, loving the Lord and our neighbor is being of service. (*Heaven and Hell* §112)

CHARITY

Since the concept of use takes such a central place in Swedenborg's view of life, the related idea of charity necessarily receives some redefinition. Swedenborg does not demean acts of charity such as giving alms to the poor, supporting the sick, and assisting the needy. Yet he questions the degree of intelligence, and even of justice, present in indiscriminate acts of charity practiced on the undeserving and the deserving alike. Motive, of course, determines the quality of the act for the individual who performs it. But society is best served by a life of continuous service through one's prime function rather than by overt benefactions that sometimes do more harm than good. To be useful and to allow everyone else the fullest possible opportunity to be useful also provides the greatest charity. All unjust, arbitrary, and artificial restraints on any individual's opportunity to live a fully useful life intrude upon the divine order of things. Swedenborg couples charity and faith. Together they lead toward a life freed from evil. The person of charity shuns evils as sins against God, but she or he does so as a matter of religious faith. Thus, Swedenborg categorically rejects faith without charity; faith alone has no place in his understanding of the order of creation.

The first step toward goodwill is not to do evil to our neighbor. A secondary point is to do good to our neighbor. This is like a doorway to the teachings on goodwill. (*True Christianity* §435)

A life of caring, though, consists of having goodwill toward our neighbors and doing good things for them; basing all of our actions on what is right and fair, and what is good and true; and applying the same principles in all our responsibilities. In a word, a life of caring consists of being useful. (*New Jerusalem* §124)

People who have charity inside, that is, love for their neighbor ... look at the enjoyment of pleasure solely in terms of its usefulness. Charity, after all, is nothing without the work of charity. Charity consists in doing—in being useful, in other words. If we love our neighbor as ourselves, we do not feel any delight in charity unless we are being active or useful. As a consequence, the life of charity is a life of usefulness. (*Secrets of Heaven* §997)

Many people believe that love for their neighbor is giving to the poor, providing means to the needy, and doing good to just anyone. In fact, true caring is acting prudently and with the intent that some good will come of it. If we provide resources to evildoers who are poor or needy, we are doing harm to our neighbors through the resources we provide, because those resources will empower the evildoers to do more evil and supply them with greater means of harming others. The situation is the opposite when we provide resources to good people. (*New Jerusalem* §100)

Common charitable efforts include spending money and labor building and maintaining public schools, orphanages, facilities for immigrants who need a place to stay, and the like. Helping poor people, widows, and orphans solely because they are poor, widows, and orphans, and giving to beggars solely because they are beggars is usefulness from an outward kind of charity. All these kinds of charity are what people call "piety." The usefulness of these acts, however, does not come from an inner kind of charity except insofar as it originates from usefulness itself and from a love for it. Outward charity without inner charity is not charity at all. Inner charity joined with outward charity creates genuine charity, since outward charity that originates from inner charity acts wisely. On the other hand, outward charity without inner charity acts foolishly and quite often ineptly. (*Draft on Divine Wisdom* §11)

Caring . . . applies to much more than just helping the poor and needy. Caring is doing what is right in everything we do, doing our duty in every position of responsibility. A judge who does what is fair for the sake of fairness is practicing caring. Judges who punish the guilty and acquit the innocent are practicing caring because in doing so they are showing concern for their fellow citizens and concern for their country. Priests who teach people truth and lead them to do good are practicing caring, if they do so for the sake of truth and goodness. If they do these things for the sake of themselves or for worldly purposes, though, they are not practicing caring, because they are loving themselves rather than their neighbor. It is the same for others whether they hold some office or not—children toward their parents, for example, and parents toward their children, servants toward their employers and employers toward their servants, subjects toward their monarch and monarchs toward their subjects. If they do their duty for the sake of duty and do what is fair for the sake of fairness, they are practicing caring. The reason all these things are related to love for our neighbor or caring is that everyone is our neighbor, . . . but to differing extents. A community, whether small or large, is more of a neighbor than an individual is, the country is still more of a neighbor, the Lord's kingdom still more, and the Lord is the neighbor above all. In the most universally applicable sense the goodness that comes from the Lord is our neighbor, and this means that what is honest and fair is our neighbor as well. So people who do anything good because it is good and who do what is honest and fair because it is honest and fair are loving their neighbor and practicing caring. This is because their actions are motivated by a love of what is good, honest, and fair and therefore by a love for people in whom there is goodness, honesty, and fairness. Caring, then, is an inner desire that makes us want to do what is good, not because we are hoping for a reward but because doing it is the joy of our life. When we are doing good as the result of an inner desire to do so, caring is present in every detail of what we are thinking and saying, what we are intending and doing. Whether we are angels or people [still on earth], if we hold goodness to be our neighbor, it can be said that in respect to our deeper natures we have become caring itself. That shows how far caring is able to go. (*New Jerusalem* §§101–4)

When we honestly, fairly, and faithfully do the work required by our job or position because we care about the work and enjoy doing it, we are continually doing what is good and useful, not only for the community or public, but also for particular individuals and private citizens. However, this is not possible unless we look to the Lord and avoid evil as a moral offense.... The good we then do is truly useful, and we do it every day.... There is a deep desire that abides inside us and wants to do good. This is how we can keep doing what is good and useful, from morning to evening, year in and year out, from the beginning to the end of life. There is no other way for us to become embodiments of goodwill. (*Sketch on Goodwill* §158)

If [business people] look to the Lord and avoid evil as a moral offense, and they conduct their business honestly, fairly, and faithfully, they embody charity. They act from what seems like their own good sense, but continually trust divine providence. Therefore, they are not depressed when they meet misfortune, nor are they filled with pride when they are successful. They think about what's ahead, but at the same time do not think about it. They think about it in terms of what they have to do and how, but they do not think about it because they yield the future to divine providence, instead of to their own judgment. They even yield their own judgment to providence. Doing business is the thing they love most about their job, and they value money as a tool for accomplishing it. . . . So, they love the work, which in itself is a useful service. They do not love the means more than the work. . . . They care about the common good while also caring about their own benefit. (*Sketch on Goodwill* §167)

Business people who act with honesty and without fraudulence are caring for the neighbor they do business with. So are workers and craftspeople when they do their work uprightly and honestly rather than falsely or deceptively. The same goes for everyone else—for ship captains and sailors, for farm workers and servants. This is goodwill itself because it can be defined as follows: goodwill is doing good to our neighbor daily and constantly—not only to our neighbor as an individual but also to our neighbor collectively. The only way to do this is through practicing goodness and justice in our position and work and with the people with whom we have any interaction, because these are things we do every day. . . . Justice and faithfulness shape their minds and the practice of goodwill shapes their bodies. Over time, because of their form, they get to the point where everything they want and think about relates to goodwill. (*True Christianity* §§422–23)

There are also many personal obligations related to goodwill, such as paying workers, paying interest on loans, honoring agreements, taking care of deposited valuables, and other things like that. Some . . . fall under criminal law, some fall under domestic law, and some fall under moral law. . . . People who have goodwill fulfill these obligations justly and faithfully. . . . The same obligations are fulfilled quite differently by people who have no goodwill. (*True Christianity* §432)

Charity means love for our neighbor. It means mercy too, since if we love our neighbors as we do ourselves we have mercy on them when they are suffering. (*Secrets of Heaven* §351)

The Word teaches nothing but the need for each of us to live in charity with our neighbor and to love the Lord above all. People who do this have deeper dimensions inside. (*Secrets of Heaven* §1408)

Since earliest times people have debated whether charity or faith is the church's firstborn. . . . People debated the subject because they did not know (any more than people do today) that the amount of charity we have determines how much faith we have. When we are being reborn, charity runs to meet faith or, to put the same thing another way, goodness runs to meet truth; it introduces itself into all aspects of faith, molds itself to fit, and causes faith to *be* faith. So charity is the church's true firstborn, even if it seems otherwise to us. (*Secrets of Heaven* §2435)

Goodwill, which in its essence is a desire to know, understand, wish for, and act on what is true, does not come to our awareness at all before forming itself in our thought (which comes from our understanding). Then, it sets itself up under a different form or appearance, which makes it visible to our inner sight. This is because sincerely thinking that something is a certain way is called faith. So, it fits that charity actually comes first and faith afterward, just as good actually comes first and truth afterward, and just as the production process must come before the product. . . . This is because goodwill comes from the Lord, and is also formed first in the spiritual mind. However, since goodwill is not apparent to us before it becomes faith, it can be said that we do not have faith until it becomes goodwill in form. The two arise at the same moment. Although goodwill produces faith, it is impossible to separate one from the other, because together they become one. . . . Faith disconnected from our way of life is not alive, and anything that is not alive—that is, dead—does not save anyone. (*Revelation Explained* §§795, 796)

This happens when we send charity into exile and extinguish it, which shatters the bond between the Lord and us. Only charity, which is love and mercy, maintains the bond. Faith without charity is incapable of doing so. . . . Can there be a person with judgment so unsound as to believe that a memorized faith can have any effect by itself? Or that mere thought based on that faith can have any effect? On the contrary, we all know from our own experience that no one can tell the real value of another's statements and assertions if they do not arise from the will or from genuine intent. It is the will and intention that please us and connect us to one another. Our real identity is whatever we will, not what we think or say without willing it. Our will is what determines our nature and character, because it is the will that has an effect. If on the other hand our thoughts are good, then the essence of faith, which is charity, lies inside the thought, because goodwill is present. But if we say our thoughts are good, while we live an evil life, we can never desire anything but evil, in which case faith is out of the question. (*Secrets of Heaven* §379)

Genuine, living goodwill does not exist unless it accompanies faith and unless both goodwill and faith jointly focus on the Lord. . . . The Lord, goodwill, and faith . . . are the three essential elements for salvation. When they are united, goodwill is goodwill, faith is faith, and the Lord is in them both and they are in the Lord. . . . When these three elements are not united, goodwill is illegitimate, hypocritical, or dead. (*True Christianity* §450)

CIVIL AFFAIRS

Swedenborg's message deals with the practical matters of everyday human relations as well as with the grander aspects of existence. Many passages contain generalizations about the proper organization and structure of life in the natural world and about the role that individuals should play in pursuit of life, liberty, and happiness for all. While civil questions belong to the most external plane of human existence, they provide the base for moral and spiritual order. Any person who loves proper civil order for its own sake and seeks to maintain individual freedom comes eventually to support the kingdom of the heavens. Humanity can scarcely become spiritual without being active in the business of life on the external plane.

In human society, there need to be two arenas of governmental order—one that is concerned with heavenly matters, and another that is concerned with worldly matters. The governance concerned with heavenly matters is called "ecclesiastical," and the governance concerned with worldly matters is called "civil."

Good order cannot be maintained in the world without officials who are required to . . . reward people who live properly and penalize people who live improperly. If this is not done, the human race will perish, since everyone has by heredity an innate desire to rule over others and to gain possession of their goods, which gives rise to hostility, envy, hatred, vengefulness, guile, cruelty, and any number of other evils. So we need to be kept under restraint by laws. Those of us who do what is good need to receive rewards that accord with our love of honors and of financial gain. Those of us who do what is evil need to receive punishments that affect those same loves (namely, loss of honor, wealth, and life). Otherwise the human race would perish. So there need to be officials to keep society in order—people who are skilled in the law, wise, and God-fearing. The officials also need their own organizational structure to prevent any of them, on some whim or out of ignorance, from allowing evils to occur that violate and therefore destroy proper order. This is guarded against when there are higher and lower officials in a hierarchical structure. (*New Jerusalem* §§311–13)

As priests are officials in charge of matters of divine law and worship, so monarchs and magistrates are in charge of matters of civil law and judgment. Since the monarch cannot administer everything alone, there need to be officials under him or her, each with a particular area of responsibility that the monarch does not have the skills or the ability to manage. These officials, taken as a whole, are the royal government, but the monarch is the highest among them. Royal majesty does not belong to the individual but is appended to her or him. Kings and queens who believe that royal majesty is intrinsic to themselves, and officials who believe that the dignity of their rank is intrinsic to themselves, are lacking in wisdom. Royal governance consists in conducting administration according to the laws of the realm and in delivering judgments in accord with those laws with an eye toward justice.... Monarchs who regard the laws as higher than themselves ascribe the royal governing to the law, and allow the law to rule over themselves. They know that the law is justice and all justice . . . is divine. Monarchs who see themselves as above the law, though, ascribe the royal governing to themselves. They believe either that they themselves are the law or that the law . . . comes from them. So they claim for themselves something that is divine, when they should be subject to it. The law . . . should be enacted . . . by individuals who are skilled in the law, wise, and God-fearing, and thereafter the monarch and subjects should live by that law. Monarchs who live by the duly enacted law set an example for their subjects by doing so. They are true monarchs. There are monarchs with absolute power, who regard their subjects as slaves, so much so that they as monarchs have a right to their subjects' possessions and even lives. If they exercise this right, they are not monarchs but tyrants. A monarch is to be obeyed as the laws of the realm prescribe and is not to be harmed in any way by deed or word. The security of the nation depends on this. (*New Jerusalem* §§319–25)

The fact that people are "the neighbor" is well known. Our community is also the neighbor because a community taken all together is a human. Our country is the neighbor because a country is made up of many communities, and is therefore a human made up of even more parts. Humankind is the neighbor because humankind is made up of large communities, each of which is a human when taken as a whole. (*Sketch on Goodwill* §72)

Our country is our neighbor more than our community is, because our country consists of many communities. Love for our country is therefore broader and higher. Loving our country is also loving the well-being of the general public. Our country is our neighbor because it is like a parent. We were born in it. It has nourished us and continues to nourish us. It has kept us safe from harm and continues to do so. We are to do good to our country with love according to what it needs. Some of its needs are earthly and some are spiritual. Its earthly needs center on its civic life and order. Its spiritual needs center on its spiritual life and order. We are to love our country not merely as much as we love ourselves; we are to love it more. There is a law written on the human heart that gives rise to the statement all just people say when they are in imminent danger of dying because of an enemy or some other cause. They say that it is a noble thing to die for their country. They say that it is a glorious thing for soldiers to shed their blood for their country. They say this because that is how much one ought to love one's country. (*True Christianity* §414)

As long as [soldiers] look to the Lord and avoid evil because it is against God, as well as do their work honestly, fairly, and faithfully, they too become charity.... In that case, they oppose needless plundering and detest needless spilling of blood. It is different in battle, though. In that environment, they are not opposed to plundering and bloodshed, because they do not think of it the same way. They think an enemy is an enemy—someone who wants their blood. When they receive orders to withdraw, they come out of this rage. After the victory, they view their prisoners as neighbors, according to the kind of good the prisoners possess. Before the battle, the soldiers raise their spirit to the Lord and put their life in his hands. Having done this, their spirit descends back to their body, and they grow courageous. Without their knowing it, the thought of the Lord remains in their spirit behind their courage. Then, if they die, they die in the Lord; if they live, they live in the Lord. (*Sketch on Goodwill* §166)

Public obligations that are related to goodwill are primarily the paying of taxes. These taxes are not to be confused with obligations connected with our jobs. Spiritual people pay their taxes with a different feeling at heart than people who are merely earthly. Spiritual people pay taxes in a spirit of goodwill, because the taxes are collected to preserve the country and protect both it and the church. The taxes also pay for administration by government officials whose salaries and stipends have to be paid out of the public treasury. Therefore people who hold their country and their church as their neighbor pay taxes uncoerced, of their own free will, and consider it wrong to cheat or avoid them. People who do not hold their country or church as their neighbor, on the other hand, perform their tax-paying obligations unwillingly and with resistance. As often as the opportunity arises, they cheat and conceal their assets. (*True Christianity* §430)

Everyone is predestined to heaven and no one to hell. We are all born human, which means that we have the image of God within us. The image of God within us is our ability to discern what is true and to do what is good. Our ability to discern what is true comes from divine wisdom and our ability to do what is good comes from divine love. This ability is the image of God; it is enduring with everyone who is whole. . . . It is why we can become civic, moral individuals; and if we can become civic and moral individuals, we can become spiritual individuals, since civic and moral life is receptive of spiritual life. We are called civic individuals if we know and abide by the laws of the country we are living in. We are called moral individuals if we make habits and virtues of these laws and live by them for rational reasons. . . . Live by these laws not only as civic and moral laws but also as divine laws and you will be a spiritual person. There is hardly a nation so barbaric that it does not have laws forbidding murder, promiscuity with other people's spouses, theft, perjury, and violation of others' rights. Civic and moral individuals keep these laws in order to be . . . good citizens. (*Divine Providence* §322)

People who in this world love the good of their country more than their own and the good of their neighbor as their own . . . love and seek the kingdom of the Lord in the other life, since there the kingdom of the Lord takes the place of one's country. Further, people who love to do good to others not for self-centered reasons but for the sake of the good itself are people who love their neighbor, since in the other life the good is one's neighbor. All individuals who are of this quality are in the universal human—that is, in heaven. (*Heaven and Hell* §64)

MORALITY

Swedenborg's teachings on morality are consistent with the great moral teachings of human history. But he emphasizes that a civil moral life should be grounded in religious convictions that presume spiritual causes. Some of his most pointed and, at the same time, felicitous phrases set forth the principles of a highly ethical life. He wrote them within the context of the rather loose morality of the eighteenth century. His family connections, wealth, education, and public offices gave him access to a wide circle of European upper-class life. Swedenborg observed the varieties of immorality that were then in vogue and wrote about them with keen insight. But all available evidence indicates that Swedenborg's own life epitomized his moral teachings.

There are three kinds of true elements: civic, moral, and spiritual. Civic truths have to do with judicial matters and the governmental affairs of nations—in general, with what is fair and equitable. Moral truths have to do with matters of personal life in its societal and social contexts, in general with what is honest and upright, and in particular with all kinds of virtues. Spiritual truths, however, have to do with matters of heaven and the church, in general with what is good in respect to love and what is true in respect to faith. (*Heaven and Hell* §468)

The laws of spiritual life, the laws of civil life, and the laws of moral life are handed down to us in the Ten Commandments. The first three commandments contain the laws of spiritual life, the next four the laws of civil life, and the last three the laws of moral life. Outwardly, purely natural people live by these same commandments just the way spiritual people do. They worship the Divine, go to church, listen to sermons, wear devout faces, do not kill or commit adultery or steal or bear false witness, do not cheat their colleagues of their goods. However, they behave this way solely in their own interest, in order to look good in the world. Inwardly, these same people are exactly the opposite of what they seem to be outwardly. Because at heart they deny the Divine, they play the hypocrite in their worship. In their private thinking they scoff at the holy rites of the church, believing that they serve only to restrain the simple masses. This is why they are wholly cut off from heaven. So since they are not spiritual, they are not moral or civic people either.... So if they were not bound by civil laws and the outward restraints exercised by their fears, they would kill. Because this is what they crave, it follows that they are constantly killing. Even though they do not commit adultery, still because they believe there is nothing wrong with it they are constantly adulterous.... Even though they do not steal, still since they do covet other people's assets and regard cheating and malicious devices as legally justifiable, they are constantly stealing in their minds. The same applies to the other commandments of moral life—not bearing false witness or coveting the goods of others. All who deny the Divine are like this, all who do not have some conscience based on religion. (*Heaven and Hell* §531)

Moral truth is what the Word teaches concerning our lives with those around us, which is called charity or goodwill. The good that comes from it (which is usefulness) generally relates to justice and equity, integrity and uprightness, sexual fidelity, self-control, honesty, good sense, and kindness. The opposites of these, which destroy charity, also point to the truth about moral life. Generally, these opposites include injustice and inequity, crookedness and fraud, promiscuity, lack of restraint, dishonesty, cunning, hostility, hatred, vengefulness, and ill will. These, too, can be called truths related to moral life, because everything that we believe, whether it is good or bad, we categorize as truth. . . . On the other hand, civil truth is the federal and local law on a civil level, which generally focuses on how justice should be carried out, and conversely on various acts of violence that occur. (*Draft on Divine Wisdom* §11)

The virtues relevant to humanity's moral wisdom go by various names, such as . . . sobriety, honesty, kindliness, . . . modesty, . . . accountability, and courtesy, as well as perseverance, industry, ingenuity, readiness, generosity, tolerance, nobility, energy, courage, . . . and many others besides. The spiritual virtues of humanity include a love of religion, compassion, truthfulness, faith, conscience, innocence, and many others. In general, these moral and spiritual virtues can be traced back to our love and enthusiasm for religion, for the public welfare, for the nation, for fellow citizens, for parents, for one's spouse, and for one's children. In all of them, the controlling factors are justice and judgment, justice being a matter of moral wisdom and judgment a matter of rational wisdom. (*Marriage Love* §164)

We all learn from our parents and teachers to live a moral life, that is, to behave like civil human beings. We learn to discharge the duties of an honorable life, which are related to the various virtues that constitute the essence of being honorable. We also learn to discharge these dutiful acts through the outward forms called manners. As we advance in age, we learn to add the exercise of rationality, and we use that rationality to enhance the morality of our life. The moral life in youths up to early adulthood is earthly. After that it becomes increasingly rational. People who reflect on the question can see that a moral life is the same thing as a life of goodwill, which is behaving well to our neighbor and regulating our life to keep it from being contaminated with evils. (*True Christianity* §443)

All works and deeds are matters of moral and civic life and therefore focus on what is honest and right and what is fair and equitable. What is honest and right is a matter of moral life, and what is fair and equitable is a matter of civic life. (*Heaven and Hell* §484)

When our moral life is also spiritual, it is a life of goodwill, because the practices involved in a moral life and in a life of goodwill are the same. Goodwill is wishing our neighbors well and therefore treating them well. This is also a moral way of life. (*True Christianity* §444)

Goodness and truth make up our life. Moral and civic goodness and truth make up the life of our outer self, while spiritual goodness and truth make up the life of our inner self. (*Secrets of Heaven* §9182)

There are moral individuals who keep the commandments of the second tablet of the Ten Commandments, who do not cheat, blaspheme, take vengeance, or commit adultery, and who are convinced that such behavior is evil because it is harmful to the state and therefore contrary to the laws of humanity. They also practice caring, honesty, fairness, and chastity. If they are doing these good things and turning their backs on evil things only because the latter are evil, though, and not because they are sins as well, these people are merely earthly, and in merely earthly individuals the root of the evil remains in place. (*Life* §108)

We mainly worship the Lord [through] . . . living by his commandments in the Word, which teach us . . . faith and . . . love. . . . This kind of life is a Christian life and is called a spiritual life. In contrast, living by the laws of justice and honor but not by the Lord's commandments is a civic, moral life. A civic, moral life makes us citizens of the world, but a spiritual life makes us citizens of heaven. (*Secrets of Heaven* §8257)

MARRIAGE AND SEX

No aspect of morality as the basis of spiritual life receives more extensive comment in Swedenborg's writings than does that of the proper relationship between the sexes. He advocates a monogamous marriage in which the partners love only each other and look together to the Lord for guidance in their lives. Such a marriage he terms truly conjugial[28] *and insists that marriage of this kind spans not only life on earth but also eternity. Death does not separate those who truly love each other. According to the Swedenborgian view, men and women are fundamentally different, not merely as to body and appearance but also as to mind. Masculinity stems from a nature that is basically intellectual. Femininity, on the other hand, results from inborn affectional qualities. The former looks toward wisdom, the latter toward love. Together they form a unity, each supplementing and complementing the other. Swedenborg sees the marriage relation as the basic unit of both the natural and the spiritual worlds. Through it the human race continues; from it proper order is maintained. From it also stems such progress as the human race may make, for married couples, seeking to perform uses together, fulfill the ultimate purpose of creation. Since the marriage relation is the seminary of human existence, the greatest delights and happiness are found in it. Swedenborg is surprisingly modern in his frank acceptance of the power of sex. In the second part of his work* Marriage Love, *he takes up some of the problems posed by the sensual urge. He subtitles this section "The Pleasures of Insanity Pertaining to Scortatory Love." In it he continues to hold up the ideal of a truly monogamous marriage untarnished by other affixations. Yet his realistic view recognizes problem areas and accepts categories of individual permission to vary from the ideal. Such variances are not set forth as equally valid substitutes for the ideal, but as sometimes permissive departures from it.*

The male is primarily a creature of intellect and the female a creature of will. . . . The male is born with an enthusiasm to learn, to understand, and to become wise, and the female with a desire to unite herself with that tendency in the male. Further, since inner qualities shape outward qualities in their own likeness, and since the masculine form is in the shape of the intellect and the feminine form is in the shape of the love of that intellect, the male has a face, voice, and body that are different from those of the female. He has a tougher face, a harsher voice, and a stronger body—

indeed, he is bearded and generally less attractive than the female. And then there are the differences in mannerisms and behavior. In short, they are not the least alike, and yet there is in every fiber an eagerness to unite. (*Marriage Love* §33)

A person does not have the smallest particle of thought, the slightest stir of feeling or activity, that does not involve a kind of marriage between intellect and will. Without some kind of marriage, nothing at all is ever produced or comes into existence. The actual organic substances of which we are made, whether taken together or separately, even down to their simplest forms, have in them both a passive and an active nature. If the passive and active did not join together in something that resembles the marriage between a husband and wife, they could not possibly exist in those substances, much less produce anything. This is true throughout the world of nature. These enduring unions trace their origin and source to the heavenly marriage, which stamps every entity in all of creation, animate or inanimate, with a picture of the Lord's kingdom. (*Secrets of Heaven* §718)

The reason a wife cannot assume the duties proper to her husband or a husband the duties proper to his wife is that they are as different as wisdom and its love, as different as thought and its feeling, as different as understanding and its will. Understanding, thought, and wisdom play the leading role in the duties proper to husbands, while will, feeling, and love play a leading role in the duties proper to wives. A wife performs her duties on the basis of the latter, while a husband performs his duties on the basis of the former. This means that their duties are different by their very nature, but they still fit together in a coherent sequence. Many people believe that women can discharge men's duties if they have been initiated into them early in life the way boys are. Women can indeed be initiated into the performance of those duties, but not into the kind of judgment on which the deeper integrity of those duties depends. So such women who have been initiated into duties appropriate to men are obliged to consult men in matters that require this kind of judgment. At that point, if it is up to them, they choose the option that is in accord with their love. . . . The reason for men's inability to assume duties appropriate to women and discharge them properly is that men cannot have women's feelings for those duties, which are quite different from men's feelings. (*Marriage Love* §175)

The inclination to bring one's spouse into unity with oneself is steady and enduring in a married woman, but it is inconsistent and variable in intensity in a married man. . . . Love cannot help loving . . . in order to be loved in return. That is its whole essence and life. Women are born to embody love, while the men with whom they unite so they can find love in return are born to embody the reception of love. Further, love is constantly at work. It is like heat, flame, and fire, which die out if they are prevented from burning. That is why a wife's inclination to bring her husband into unity with herself is steady and enduring. The reason a husband's inclination toward his wife is not the same is that a husband is not an embodiment of love but simply a receiver of love. His receptivity comes and goes depending on other concerns that may affect it, on ups and downs from various causes in the warmth of his thinking, and on the waxing and waning of his physical energies. (*Marriage Love* §160)

No wife loves her husband because of the way he looks but because of the intelligence he displays in his work and in the way he behaves.... Wives unite themselves with their husbands' intelligence and this is how they unite with their husbands, so if a man loves himself because of his intelligence he is withdrawing this love from his wife and keeping it for himself. This brings about disunion rather than oneness. Not only that, loving one's own intelligence is claiming to be wise on one's own account, which is madness, and so it is loving one's own madness. (*Marriage Love* §331)

The marital relationship between one husband and one wife is the jewel of human life. (*Marriage Love* §457)

Marriage love is the basis for all love. (*Secrets of Heaven* §4280)

The most perfect, the noblest human form occurs when two forms become one form through marriage, or when two fleshes become one.... Now the husband's mind is raised into a higher light and a wife's mind into a higher warmth, and now they can sprout, flower, and bear fruit like trees in spring.... Noble fruits are born out of the nobility of that form—spiritual fruits in the heavens and earthly fruits on earth. (*Marriage Love* §201)

[Married love seen in the light of] its origin ... is heavenly, spiritual, holy, pure, and clean beyond any other kind of love from the Lord that exists with the angels in heaven or with humans. (*Marriage Love* §64)

I realize that not many people are going to recognize that all kinds of joy and pleasure, from the first to the last, are incorporated into marriage love, for the simple reason that the genuine marriage love into which they are incorporated is so rare nowadays that people do not know what it is. They scarcely realize that it exists. . . . They are not incorporated into any other sort of marriage love but genuine marriage love. Since this is so rare on earth, the only way to describe its surpassing happiness is out of the mouths of angels. . . . Its deepest pleasures are pleasures of the soul, where the marital inclination between love and wisdom, or between goodness and truth, first flows from the Lord. They are imperceptible and therefore indescribable because they are pleasures of peace and innocence combined. . . . As they descend they become more and more perceptible. On the higher levels of the mind they are experienced as bliss, lower down in the mind as happiness, and in the heart as the kind of enjoyment one gets from these. They spread out from the heart into each and every part of the body, eventually combining into the ultimate pleasure in the outermost parts of the body. (*Marriage Love* §69)

As for a love for the opposite sex, we all have this in common. At our creation it was implanted in our very soul, which is the source of our whole being, for the sake of the propagation of the human race. (*Marriage Love* §46)

The desire for the opposite sex in humans is not the origin of marriage love, but it is its first phase, acting as an outward or earthly ground in which something inward or spiritual can be sown. . . . Genuine marriage love is found only among ardent seekers of wisdom who therefore keep making steady progress toward it. The Lord anticipates their need and provides them with marriage love. This love does begin with a desire for the opposite sex or, better yet, *through* a desire for the opposite sex, but that is still not its origin. . . . Wisdom and this love are inseparable partners. Marriage love begins *through* a desire for the opposite sex because before a partner is found, we desire the other sex in general, look upon members of it with an affectionate eye, and treat them with courteous morality. The young man is in the process of choosing, and . . . his outward being feels a gentle warming because of an inherent predisposition toward marriage with one woman that lies hidden within the recesses of his mind. Further, . . . the decision to marry can be delayed for various reasons until well into adulthood, and . . . in this interim the beginnings of that desire are experienced as lust. . . . This applies to those of the masculine sex, though, since the attraction they experience is one by which they are aroused to act. I am not referring to the female sex. . . . Desire for the opposite sex is not the origin of genuine marriage love. Rather, it comes first in time but not in importance. (*Marriage Love* §98)

The general desire for the opposite sex is a desire directed toward and involving more than one member of the opposite sex, while marriage love is directed solely toward and involves only one member of the opposite sex. Desire directed toward and involving more than one is an earthly desire that we have in common with beasts and birds, who are merely natural; while marriage love is a spiritual desire, uniquely and essentially human because humans were created to become spiritual and are therefore born to become spiritual. As a result, to the extent that we do become spiritual, we shed our general desire for the opposite sex and take up marriage love. At the beginning of a marriage, desire for the opposite sex seems bound up with marriage love, but as the marriage progresses, that desire and marriage love diverge. Then, in the case of people who are spiritual, general desire for the opposite sex is expelled from them and a love of marriage is infused into them. In the case of people who are earthly, the opposite happens. (*Marriage Love* §48)

Desire for the opposite sex is found in an earthly person, whereas marriage love is found in a spiritual person. An earthly person desires and longs only for superficial union and the physical pleasures that go with it, but a spiritual person desires and longs for a deeper connection and for the accompanying well-being of the spirit. The spiritual person realizes that this can happen only with one spouse, a spouse with whom one can be continually more and more united into one person. There is an increasing sense of well-being the more closely the spouses are joined, and this continues to eternity. The earthly person, however, does not think this way. (*Marriage Love* §38)

Genuine marriage love is not possible between one husband and more than one wife. Polygamy in fact destroys the spiritual source of marriage love, whose purpose is to form one mind out of two. It therefore destroys the deeper union of the good and the true that is the very essence of that love. Marriage with more than one is like an intellect divided among more than one will. (*Heaven and Hell* §379)

Engagement serves to unite one mind to the other, so that there is a marriage of the spirit before the marriage of the body. (*Marriage Love* §303)

Marriage is intrinsically spiritual and therefore holy. It comes down to us from the heavenly marriage of goodness and truth, and the various features of marriage reflect the divine marriage of the Lord and the church. As a result, those features actually come from the Lord.... Since ... the ordained clergy administers the Lord's priestly functions on earth, that is, matters relating to his love and therefore his blessing, it is right and proper that marriages should actually be blessed by his ministers. In addition, marriages should be blessed by clergypersons because they are in fact the principal witnesses. They should also hear, approve, and affirm the consent to the contract, and in this way make it an established fact. (*Marriage Love* §308)

The first state of love between married partners is one of warmth not yet moderated by light, but ... it can be gradually moderated if the husband becomes more accomplished in wisdom and the wife comes to love that wisdom in her husband. (*Marriage Love* §145)

This [is] accomplished through the useful service they each perform ... with one another's help, and the pleasure ... then mount[s] in accordance with the balance of warmth and light, or of wisdom and the love of wisdom. (*Marriage Love* §137)

The joy of living together increases for people who are committed to a true love of marriage, but it decreases for [married] people who are not committed to a true love of marriage.... People who are committed to a true love of marriage ... love each other with all their senses. Nothing is more pleasant for a wife to look at than her husband, and nothing is more pleasant for him to look at than her.... They find nothing more pleasant than the sound, smell, or touch of each other, which leads to joy in the household, the bedroom, and the bed. (*Marriage Love* §213)

Anything done in a spirit of true marriage love is done in a spirit of mutual freedom, because all freedom comes of love. Both partners are free when each loves what the other thinks and what the other wills. That is why a desire for control in the marriage destroys genuine love, removing the freedom inherent in love and therefore the pleasure too. The pleasure in control that replaces it breeds discord, alienates hearts, and sows evil, depending on how domineering the one party is and how submissive the other. . . . A marriage is sacred and to injure it is to injure something holy. Adultery is therefore profane, because just as the pleasure of marriage love descends from heaven, the pleasure of adultery ascends from hell. (*Secrets of Heaven* §§10173, 10174)

Anyone who has lived in a truly loving marriage has no desire to remarry, unless she or he has reasons to do so that are unrelated to marriage love. . . . Such people have become unified in soul and therefore in mind, and since this is a spiritual unification, it is truly a bonding of one person's soul and mind to those of the other, a bond that can in no way be dissolved. . . . They are united physically when the propagations of the husband's soul are received by the wife, and in this way his life is implanted in hers. This transforms a [mere] young woman into a wife. . . . When the husband receives marriage love from his wife, it disposes the deeper parts of his mind—and his body, both inside and out—into a state that is open to love and sensitive to wisdom. This state changes him from a [mere] young man into a husband. . . .

An aura of love is constantly emanating from the wife and an aura of intellect from the husband, and this joins them ever more closely together. (*Marriage Love* §321)

We cannot know the true nature of the chastity of marriage if we do not turn our backs on the lechery of adultery as a sin. . . . The lechery of adultery and the chastity of marriage are as different from each other as hell and heaven are from each other, and that the lechery of adultery makes hell for us and the chastity of marriage makes heaven for us. (*Life* §76)

Sensory-minded people in their delusion believe that adultery is fine. They decide on the basis of their senses that marriage exists merely to provide for the orderly raising of children. As long as this arrangement is not destroyed, they think, it does not matter who produces the children. They also believe that the marital urge is like any other lust except for being allowable. . . . There is a correspondence between the heavenly marriage and marriage on earth, that we have no capacity for marriage unless we commit ourselves to spiritual truth and goodness, that a real marriage cannot exist between a husband and many wives, and that marriage is therefore inherently sacred. . . . When our senses hold the power in us, . . . we live in thick darkness, and we then believe that every conclusion to which our senses lead us is a rational one. (*Secrets of Heaven* §5084)

Fornication derives from our desire for the opposite sex. . . . Desire for the opposite sex is like the spring from which both marriage love and promiscuous desire may flow. . . . Desire for the opposite sex is inherent in everyone, whether it is expressed or not. Its expression with a sexually available woman before marriage is called fornication. Its expression only with a wife and not before is called marriage. Its expression with another woman after marriage is called adultery. So . . . a desire for the opposite sex is like a spring from which both chaste and unchaste love can well up. . . . Can anyone claim that a person who has committed fornication has lost the ability to become more chaste after he marries? Fornication derives from the desire for the opposite sex. . . . This desire begins when a young man starts to think and act on his own understanding, and his voice begins to sound masculine. There is a shift in our minds during this period: previously we had based our thinking only on concepts stored in our memory, reflecting on them and following them. . . . But now, led by our love, we arrange the concepts stored in our memory in a new order and manage our own lives accordingly. We gradually come to think more and more in keeping with our own rationality and to exercise our own free will. . . . Desire for the opposite sex follows on the beginning of our ability to understand things for ourselves, and it develops as that understanding gains strength. . . . It is wisdom to restrain desire for the opposite sex and insanity to give it latitude. (*Marriage Love* §§445–46)

Of course, it is better if [the spring of a man's virility] is impounded [for a wife], but if [this] is impossible because of the unbridled strength of their urge, a temporary solution may be sought to prevent marriage love from perishing in the interim. . . . Hiring a lover may be the solution. . . . It serves to check and limit indiscriminate, misplaced fornication, and thus leads to a more disciplined state that is more akin to married life. . . . The sexual ardor that boils up and seems to burn in the first phase of early adulthood can be calmed and eased, and the foul lust of an intense sexual drive can be tempered by something that at least resembles marriage. . . . All this does not apply, though, to men who are capable of keeping their urges from boiling over or who can marry as soon as they become physically capable of it, offering and devoting to their wives the first fruits of their virility. (*Marriage Love* §459)

The marital relationship between one husband and one wife is the jewel of human life. . . . Marriage love is the setting and source of the heavenly blessings, spiritual joys, and consequent earthly pleasures that have been intended from the beginning for people who are committed to a true marriage love. . . . Marriage love is the foundation of all heavenly and spiritual loves and therefore all earthly loves, and . . . all joys and delights from the first to the last are gathered into this love. (*Marriage Love* §457)

THE NATURE OF WISDOM

The Swedenborgian conception of the nature of creation rests upon belief in the inviolability of human freedom. Humanity can use this freedom for ends that conform to or deny the divine pattern; otherwise, this freedom would not be genuine. Yet within the divinely given freedom, God hopes humanity will apply itself to wisdom. Swedenborg defines wisdom as the welding of good and truth in support of use. Some of the more abstruse aspects of the Swedenborgian view of life may be found in his comments on the human mind, how it receives influx from the spiritual world and how it arrives at decisions. The selections that follow were chosen to provide an introduction to

Swedenborg's ideas concerning the difficult subject of the nature of wisdom, a subject that philosophers and theologians have argued through the centuries.

It is part of the divine design that we act in freedom and according to reason, because acting in freedom according to reason is acting on our own. However, these two powers, freedom and reason, are not our own. They are the Lord's within us; and since we are human they are not taken from us, because we cannot be reformed without them. That is, we cannot practice repentance, we cannot fight against evils and as a result bear fruit that is consistent with repentance. . . . So since we are given freedom and reason by the Lord and we act from them, it follows that we are not acting on our own but as though we were on our own. (*Life* §101)

There are three things that belong together and that cannot be separated: love, wisdom, and useful living. If one of these is taken away, the other two collapse. (*Revelation Unveiled* §352)

No one, though, should believe that we have wisdom if we know a lot, grasp what we know fairly clearly, and can talk about things intelligently. We are wise only if these abilities are united to love. Love is what produces wisdom, through its desires. If wisdom is not united to love it is like a meteor in the sky that vanishes, like a falling star. Wisdom united to love is like the constant light of the sun and like a fixed star. We have a love for wisdom to the extent that we fight off the demonic horde—our cravings for whatever is evil and false. (*Divine Providence* §35)

The earthly level holds facts of various kinds. There are facts about earthly, bodily, and worldly matters, which are the lowliest kind, since they come directly from the evidence of the outward, physical senses. There are facts about the civil realm and the government, statutes, and laws of the state; and these are a little deeper. There are facts about the issues of moral life, which are even deeper. But facts about spiritual life are deeper than all the others. These are the church's truths. As long as we know them only from theology, they are mere facts, but when they come from a loving goodness, they soar above facts, because they then dwell in spiritual light. From that vantage point, they see facts laid out in order below them. By these steps—different levels of fact—we climb to a point of understanding, because facts on their different levels open our mind, enabling light from the spiritual world to flow in. (*Secrets of Heaven* §5934)

From infancy to the end of our life in the world, we improve in understanding and wisdom, and if all is to be well with us, we must also improve in faith and love. It is mainly facts that serve this cause. Facts are absorbed as we listen, observe, and read, and are stored away in our outer, earthly memory. They serve our inner eye, or intellect, as a field of objects from which to select and elect those that help us develop wisdom. Our inner eye or intellect, you see, uses its proper light (which comes from heaven) to gaze down on that field (that part of the memory) and select and elect from the various items there the kinds of facts that suit its passions. These facts it summons from the outer memory and stores in its ... inner memory. ... That is what brings the inner self its life, its understanding, and its wisdom. (*Secrets of Heaven* §9723)

Young people still in their adolescence cannot think on any more profound plane than the outer earthly level, because they cobble their thoughts together from sense impressions. As they grow up and use what they learn from their senses to figure out the causes of things, they start thinking on an inner earthly level. They are then fashioning a certain amount of truth out of sense impressions, and this truth ventures beyond the senses, but it still remains within the earthly realm. Once they mature into young adults, they might cultivate the ability to reason. If so, they are using the contents of the earthly plane to develop rational ideas, which are a still more elevated form of truth, abstracted from the contents of the inner earthly plane. The scholarly world refers to thoughts with these underpinnings as intuitive, immaterial ideas. Ideas based on facts belonging to both earthly planes are called material ideas, though, so far as they partake of the world and draw on the senses. It is by our intellect, then, that we climb from earth toward heaven. Still, intellect does not bring us into heaven unless we take in the good from the Lord that is constantly present, exerting its influence. If we take the good in, we also receive truth as a gift, since all truth lodges in goodness, and as we receive truth, we also receive the gift of intellect, which puts us in heaven. (*Secrets of Heaven* §5497)

People are not people because they have a human face and body—they are people because they have wisdom in their intellect and goodness in their will. The higher the quality of this wisdom and goodness, the more human the people are. When people are born they are more brutish than any animal. They become human through being instructed. If they are responsive to the instruction, a mind forms within them. People are human because of their mind, depending on its particular nature. There are animals that have faces that are close to human, but they have no faculty for higher understanding or for taking any action on the basis of that understanding. They act on an instinct that is activated by their earthly love. . . . Animals express in sound the feelings belonging to their love, while people speak their feelings as transferred into thought. Animals turn their faces downward and look at the ground, while people look at the sky in all directions, their faces lifted up. From these points we can draw the following conclusion: the more we base what we say on sound reasoning and the more we focus on the time we will spend in heaven, the more human we are. Conversely, the more we base what we say on twisted reasoning and focus only on the time we are to spend in the world, the less human we are. In the latter case, we are still human, but only potentially rather than actually, since all people have the power to understand things that are true and to intend actions that are good. Even if we have no intention of doing what is good or understanding what is true, we nonetheless retain the ability to ape and mimic human qualities on the outside. (*True Christianity* §417)

The importance of knowing truth and believing it, then, is crystal clear, since truth enlightens us and falsity blinds us. Truth opens up to the rational mind a field that is immeasurable and almost unbounded. Falsity by comparison opens hardly any field at all, even if the appearance is otherwise. That is why angels' wisdom is so vast—because they possess truth. Truth, after all, is the light itself of heaven. (*Secrets of Heaven* §2588)

People who learn truths and do not live by them are like people who scatter seeds on top of a field but do not plow them under—the seeds become swollen by the rain and split into empty husks. People who learn truths and do them are like people who sow and plow the seeds under. With the benefit of rain, the seeds then grow into a harvest and become useful for nutrition. (*True Christianity* §347)

Nevertheless, sense-centered people can think logically, some of them actually with more skill and penetration than other people. However, they rely on deceptive sensory appearances bolstered by their own learning, and since they can think logically in this fashion, they think they are wiser than other people. The fire that fuels their reasoning is the fire of love for themselves and the world. (*Heaven and Hell* §353)

We all have a capacity for understanding and wisdom, but some of us are wiser than others, because we do not equally ascribe to the Lord all understanding and wisdom.... People who ascribe all of it to the Lord are wiser than the rest of us, because all truth and goodness—the components of wisdom—flow in from heaven.... Attributing all of it to the Lord opens up our inner depths in the direction of heaven, because to attribute all of it to him is to acknowledge that nothing true or good comes from ourselves. The more we acknowledge this, the more we bid farewell to self-love and to the darkness generated by falsity and evil, which departs along with self-love. We also enter more and more into innocence and into love for and faith in the Lord. As a result we are united with the Deity, influenced by him, and enlightened. . . . All of us equally have a capacity for [wisdom; however, we] do not all have an equal capacity for wisdom. . . . An aptitude for wisdom does not mean an aptitude for debating about truth and goodness on the basis of facts nor consequently for proving whatever one wishes. No, it means an ability to discern what is true and good, choose what is most fitting, and apply it to the purposes one serves in life. People who credit everything to the Lord are the ones who discern, choose, and apply. Conversely, people who give the credit not to the Lord but to themselves know only how to debate about truth and goodness. The only insights they have actually belong to others. . . . They are unable to peer into actual truth, so they stand outside and confirm whatever they seize on, whether it is true or false. When people are able to do this through an especially erudite use of facts, the world considers them wiser than others. The more they attribute everything to themselves, though, and accordingly love what they themselves think up, the crazier they are. They support falsity over truth, and evil over what is good. This is because their only sources of light are illusions and appearances existing in the material world. So they rely on their own illumination (called worldly light) separated from heaven's light, and when it is separated, that illumination is pure darkness regarding the true ideas and good qualities of heaven. (*Secrets of Heaven* §10227)

From [the Lord] comes wisdom, through wisdom comes understanding, through understanding comes reason; and reason, in turn, makes the facts we have memorized come alive. This is the proper way for the inner life to be organized. (*Secrets of Heaven* §121)

RELIGION

According to Swedenborg, life should center on religion, and the life of religion means doing good. But he did not seek a specific church organization to support his concept of religion. He believed that the form of religion meant little compared to its essence—a life of use. Thus the quality of an individual's life defines her or his true religion. Swedenborg, although convinced that God was speaking a new revelation through him, was ecumenically minded. He asserted that all people can go to heaven, provided they live a good life, in consonance with their religious beliefs. The truths given to a particular religion do, of course, affect the quality of its goods. Swedenborg looks to the ideal of ultimate acceptance of a rational faith by all. Yet his teachings allow for varied forms of religious individuality consistent with belief in a God-centered universe.

Religion Is All about How We Live, and the Religious Way to Live Is to Do Good (*Life* §§1–8)

[To glorify God] means to bear the fruits of love, that is, to perform the duties of your position in a trustworthy, honest, and reliable way. This is what it means to love God and to love our neighbor. This is what holds society together and makes it worthwhile. By this means God is to be glorified. (*Marriage Love* §9)

Everyone who has any religion knows and acknowledges that people who lead a good life are saved and people who lead an evil life are damned. That is, they know and acknowledge that if we lead a good life we think good things not only about God but also about our neighbor, which is not the case if we lead an evil life. What we love constitutes our life, and whatever we love we not only do freely but also think freely. So we say that life is doing good things because doing good things is inseparable from thinking good things. If this doing and this thinking are not working together in us, then they are not part of our life. (*Life* §1)

The quality of the volition and thought that cause the deed or work determines the quality of the deed or work. If the thought and intent are good, then the deeds and works are good; but if the thought and intent are evil, then the deeds and works are evil, even though they may look alike in outward form. A thousand people . . . can do the same thing, so much alike that in outward form one can hardly tell the difference. Yet each deed in its own right is unique because it comes from a different intent. (*Heaven and Hell* §472)

Belief in God and refusal to do evil because it is against God are the two elements that make a religion a religion. If either is lacking, we cannot call it a religion, since believing in God and doing evil are mutually contradictory, as are doing what is good and not believing in God. Neither is possible apart from the other. The Lord has provided that there should be some religion almost everywhere and that everyone who believes in God and does not do evil because it is against God should have a place in heaven. (*Divine Providence* §326)

Religion within us is made up of living according to divine precepts, which are contained in their entirety in the Ten Commandments. People who do not live according to these are not able to have religion, because they do not respect God, much less love him. Neither do they respect others, much less love them. After all, how can they respect God or others if they steal, commit adultery, kill, and lie? (*Revelation Explained* §948)

Every religion has the general principle that we are to examine ourselves, practice repentance, and refrain from sins, and if we do not do this, we suffer damnation. (*Life* §64)

We live moral lives from a place of spirituality when we live morally because of our religion. . . . When we are met with evil, dishonesty, or injustice, we think that these things just should not be done, since they are against divine law. When we avoid doing those things on account of divine law, we prepare a spiritual life for ourselves, and our moral life grows out of it. This is because people communicate with the angels of heaven through this type of faith and thought, and communication with heaven opens their internal spirituality. Their mind, then, is a higher mind, like those of the angels in heaven, and they are steeped in heavenly intelligence and wisdom. To lead a moral life from a place of spirituality is to live according to religion. People who lead moral lives for these reasons rise above their worldly selves, and thus above their ego, and are lead through heaven by the Lord. As a result, these people will have faith, respect God, have conscience, and harbor an affection for the true things of the spirit. This affection is a longing to discover the truth and goodness in the Word, because to them, these things are divine laws that they live by. . . . On the other hand, living a moral life not from a place of religion, but only because of fear of earthly law, or because of fear of a damaged reputation, or of losing praise and wealth, is living a moral life not from a spiritual place but from a material one. As a result, such people have no communication with heaven. Since these people think dishonestly and unfairly about the people around them, and yet act and speak otherwise, their inner spiritual nature is closed up. Only their inner material nature is open. This opening lets in the light of the material world, but not the light of heaven. Because of this, such people make little of the Divine and heaven, or even deny them altogether, believing that nature and the world are all there is. (*Revelation Explained* §195)

There has been religion from the earliest times and . . . people all over the world have known about God and have known something about life after death. (*Sacred Scripture* §117)

Under the Lord's divine providence, every nation has a religion. . . . Every nation that lives by its religion—that is, that does not do evil because it is against its God—is given a spiritual element within its worldly life. . . . If [an] individual says, "I was born Christian, I was baptized, I have confessed the Lord, read the Word, and taken the Holy Supper," does all this matter if this individual has a craving for murder and revenge, for adultery, surreptitious theft, perjury, lies, and all kinds of violence, and does not regard them as sins? Are people like this thinking about God or about some eternal life? Do they think that they exist? Surely sound reason tells us that people like this cannot be saved. (*Divine Providence* §322)

The general opinion is that people who have been born outside the church, the people called "the nations" or "non-Christians," cannot be saved because they do not have the Word and therefore do not know the Lord; and without the Lord there is no salvation.... However ... the Lord's mercy is universal ... [and] it is extended to all individuals. Non-Christians are born just as human as people within the church, who are in fact few by comparison. It is not their fault that they do not know the Lord. So anyone who thinks from any enlightened reason at all can see that no one is born for hell. The Lord is actually love itself, and his love is an intent to save everyone. (*Heaven and Hell* §318)

Many people outside the church live ... a moral life, because they think they should not do evil since it is against their religion. This is why so many of them are saved. (*Revelation Explained* §195)

Heaven is within us, and people who have heaven within them come into heaven. The heaven within us is our acknowledgment of the Divine and our being led by the Divine. (*Heaven and Hell* §319)

We are all born into the religion of our parents and are introduced into it in early childhood, and we remain in it afterward.... If we stay with our religion and believe in God ... and revere the Word ... and we live by the principles of the Ten Commandments ..., we will not swear allegiance to notions that are false.... We are in a position to embrace it and be led out of our former false beliefs. However, this will not happen if we have thoroughly convinced ourselves of the falsities of our religion, because once we have convinced ourselves of something false, that belief is there to stay and cannot be uprooted. Once we have convinced ourselves of something false we have in effect sworn allegiance to it, especially if it appeals to our beloved self-importance and therefore to our pride in our own wisdom. (*Sacred Scripture* §92)

It is extremely common for us to form an opinion about some religious tenet and then judge that other people cannot be saved unless they believe what we do, even though the Lord forbade this.... People of every religious persuasion are saved as long as they have acquired a remnant of goodness and seeming truth.... A life of neighborly love involves thinking well of people, wanting what is good for them, and feeling personal joy in the notion that others too are saved. (*Secrets of Heaven* §2284)

The Lord's spiritual church ... extends throughout the globe. It is not limited to people who have the Word and therefore know the Lord and some truth taught by the faith; it also exists among people who do not have the Word, are completely ignorant of the Lord as a result, and therefore do not know any of the faith's true concepts. (*Secrets of Heaven* §3263)

There are three essential principles of the church: belief in the divine nature of the Lord, belief in the holiness of the Word, and the life that we call "charity." ... If these three principles had functioned as the essential principles of the church, then intellectual dissent would not have divided it. It would only have varied it the way light varies the colors of beautiful things, and the way different gems make up the beauty of a royal crown. (*Divine Providence* §259)

Strict materialists ... say at heart, "How can there be so many contradictory religions rather than one worldwide, true religion when the goal of divine providence is a heaven from the human race ... ?" Please listen, though! No matter what religion people are born into, people can all be saved if they believe in God and live by the precepts of the Ten Commandments—not to kill, not to commit adultery, not to steal, and not to commit perjury, because to do so would be contrary to their religion and therefore contrary to God. They have a fear of God and a love for their neighbor, a fear of God because they think that committing these acts is against God and a love for their neighbor because murder, adultery, theft, perjury, and coveting their neighbor's house and spouse are against their neighbor. Because these people turn to the Lord during their lives and do no harm to their neighbors, they are led by the Lord; and people who are so led are also taught about God and their neighbor according to their religions. This is because people who live this way want to be taught, while people who live otherwise do not. Further, people who want to be taught are taught by angels after death, when they become spirits, and gladly accept the kind of truths we find in the Word. (*Divine Providence* §253)

The Christian religion has closed the door on intelligence, and the theology of faith alone has sealed it shut. Each of these erects an iron wall around itself, the wall being the dogma that theological matters are beyond our grasp and that we should therefore not use our rationality in our approach to them, that they are for the blind, not for the sighted. This hides from view the truths that teach what spiritual freedom is. (*Divine Providence* §149)

Doctrine in itself does not make the outer shell; still less does it make the inner core. . . . The Lord does not differentiate religious movements by their doctrine, either, but by the way their members live what is taught. All doctrine—if it is true doctrine—looks to a life of love as its fundamental principle. What is the point of doctrine but to teach us how to be human? In the Christian world, it is doctrine that differentiates churches. Doctrine is the basis on which people call themselves Roman Catholic, Lutheran (or Evangelical), Calvinist (or Reformed), and other names as well. These names grow out of doctrine alone, which would never happen if we considered love for the Lord and charity for our neighbor the chief concern of faith. If we did, those distinctions would simply be differences of opinion on the mysteries of faith. True Christians would leave such issues up to the individual and the individual's conscience. In their hearts they would say, "A person who lives as a Christian—who lives as the Lord teaches—is a real Christian." One church would come out of all the different churches, and all disagreement due to doctrine alone would vanish. Even the hatred of one denomination for another would melt away in a moment, and the Lord's kingdom would come on earth. (*Secrets of Heaven* §1799)

Love and charity are the essential ingredients of all theology and worship. If we took this as a premise, . . . heresy would then vanish. All the churches would join into one, no matter how great the differences in doctrinal teachings derived from this premise or pointing to it, and no matter how great the differences in ritual. . . . If this were how matters now stood, we would all be ruled as one person by the Lord. We would be like members and organs of a single body that, although they differ in form and function, are still connected to a single heart, on which they all depend, each in its own form, each different from the next. Then, no matter what our theology or what our outward form of worship, we would each say, "You are my kin; I see that you worship the Lord and that you are a good person." (*Secrets of Heaven* §2385)

As for priests, they are to teach people the way to heaven and are also to lead them on that path. They are to teach them according to the body of teaching of their church drawn from the Word and are to lead them to live by that teaching. Priests who teach what is true and who by means of truths lead people to practice goodness in their lives and therefore lead them to the Lord are good shepherds . . . ; priests who teach but do not lead people to practice goodness in their lives and therefore do not lead them to the Lord are bad shepherds. Priests must not claim to have power over people's souls, because in actuality they do not know the state of people's inner selves. It is even more important for priests not to claim the power to open and close heaven, since that power belongs to the Lord alone. Priests should be accorded dignity and honor because of the holy functions they perform; but if they are wise, they ascribe the honor not to themselves but to the Lord, who is the source of what is holy. If they are not wise, they ascribe the honor to themselves—and take it away from the

Lord. . . . None of the honor that goes with any function belongs to the individual performing it. Rather, it is appended to the individual in accord with the importance of the function being performed; and anything that is appended does not belong to the individual and is taken away from her or him when the position passes to another. The only honor that remains ours is honor we receive for our wisdom and fear of the Lord. Priests are to teach the people and to lead them by means of truths to practice goodness in their lives. Priests are not to compel anyone, though, because people cannot be compelled to believe anything that contradicts what they think in their hearts to be true. People whose beliefs differ from those of the priest but who do not cause disturbances should be left in peace. (*New Jerusalem* §§315–18)

EVIL, SIN, AND THE PERMISSIONS INVOLVED

Many modern thinkers doubt the very existence of evil and sin. Swedenborg believed otherwise. Evil and falsity exist and together lead to sin. Sin repeated becomes confirmed, and sinners eventually consign themselves to hell. Thus, Swedenborg's view of life contains great similarity to the traditional Christian concept of evil. Yet Swedenborg presents much new thought on these subjects. Evil and falsity were not part of the divine order except in the sense that humanity received true freedom to choose evil over good. Subsequently, human beings were born into tendencies toward the evils of their ancestry. Yet people do not acquire any evils except as a result of confirming them by the actions of their lives. A person does what they love and may violate order in accord with the exercise of their inborn free will. Repentance from sin may lead to regeneration of the person's basic character and to ultimate happiness in heaven. Such character regeneration comes from the Lord, but the individual must initiate the process. This initiative can stem only from a genuine desire to reform, thus from a free choice. Divine love seeks the salvation of every individual, but it permits those who will, to fail. No divine fiat could alter this without fundamentally denying the human individual an opportunity to be captain of her or his own soul.

[The same goes for the fact that Adam and Eve] were cursed because they both ate from a particular tree; and that that curse remains in effect for every human being after them, which means that the whole human race was damned for the misdeed of a single individual—and a misdeed in which there was no evil from a craving of the flesh or a wickedness of the heart. Does this square with divine justice? Why indeed did Jehovah, who was present and watching this happen, not distract Adam from eating? And why did he not throw the snake into the underworld before it exercised its persuasive powers? But . . . the reason God did not do all this is that he would have taken away human free choice by so doing, and yet freedom is what makes a human a human and not an animal. Once this is known, it becomes obvious that the two trees, one for life and the other for death, represent human free choice in spiritual matters. For another thing, hereditary evil is not from this source; it is from our parents instead. Parents pass on to their children a weakness for the evil they themselves have been involved in. Anyone can see that this is the case by carefully examining the behavior, the minds, and the faces of children . . . descended from the same ancestor. Nevertheless, it is up to each individual in the family whether he or she wishes to move toward that evil or away from it, since each one has his or her own free choice. (*True Christianity* §469)

Evil, or harm, did not exist until after the creation of the universe. (*Sketch for "True Christianity"* §9)

By turning away from God and turning toward themselves as though they were a god, they created a source of evil in themselves. (*Marriage Love* §444)

Eminence and wealth in this world are not genuine divine blessings, even though we call them that because we enjoy them so much. They . . . lead many of us astray and turn us away from heaven. No, the real blessings that come from the Divine are eternal life and the happiness it brings. . . . The reason the skills of evil people bring them success is that by the divine design, whatever we do, we do on the basis of our own reasoning and our own free will. If we did not have the freedom to act on the basis of our own reasoning, . . . we could not even begin being prepared to receive eternal life. Eternal life is instilled in us only when we are in a state of freedom and when our powers of reason are enlightened. This is because no one can be compelled by outside forces to become a good person, since nothing that is done under compulsion is of lasting effect. The goodness under that circumstance would not become ours. What is ours is what we do freely according to our own reasoning, and what we do freely is what we do because we will it and love it; our will or our love is our true self. If we are compelled to do something that we do not want to do, then our mind is constantly turning to what we would rather do instead. Not only that, everyone is drawn to what is forbidden because of the hidden pull of freedom. . . . If we were not kept in a state of freedom we could not be provided with any goodness. God's allowing us the freedom to think, intend, and (within the limits of the law) even do what is evil is called "permission." (*New Jerusalem* §§270, 271–72)

As created, love for ourselves and love for the world are heavenly loves. They are in fact loves proper to our physical self and of service to our spiritual loves the way foundations are of service to houses. It is love for ourselves and love for the world that prompt us to care about our bodies, to want nourishment, clothing, and housing, to take care of our homes, to look for jobs in order to be useful. . . . They bring us into a state of serving the Lord and the neighbor. In contrast, when there is no love for serving the Lord and the neighbor, when there is nothing but love for using the world to suit ourselves, then the love becomes hellish instead of heavenly. It makes us focus our minds and spirits on our self-image, which intrinsically is completely evil. (*Divine Love and Wisdom* §396)

[Thus perverted] the evil of self-love disconnects us not only from the Lord but also from heaven. We love no one but ourselves, and we love others only so far as we see them in ourselves, or so far as they merge with us. We make ourselves the center of everyone's attention, always diverting attention away from others and especially from the Lord. When lots of people in a single community behave this way, all of them are naturally at odds. Each member inwardly views the next as an enemy. They hate anyone who works against them in any way, and take pleasure in such a person's ruin. The evil of love for worldly advantages is no different. This evil covets the wealth and possessions of others and wants to own everything that belongs to another. This too results in hostility and hatred, though to a lesser degree. If you want to know what evil is and therefore what sin is, all you need to do is work at learning what self-love and love for worldly advantages are. If you want to know what good is, all you need to do is work at learning what love for the Lord and love for your neighbor are. (*Secrets of Heaven* §4997)

Because self-love breeds hatred, vengefulness, cruelty, and adultery, it breeds everything we call sin, crime, abomination, and profanation. When self-love is present in our rational mind, then, and in the compulsions and delusions of our outer self, the inflow of the Lord's heavenly love is constantly being choked off, twisted, and defiled. It is like a stinking heap of dung that dispels and even befouls any sweet fragrance. It is also like a physical object that takes the rays of light steadily streaming into it and turns them into horrible, dark colors. Again, it is like a tiger or snake that rebuffs the kindly words of its feeders and kills them by tooth or fang. Or it is like a misanthrope who takes even the best intentions of other people and their very deeds of kindness and interprets them as insults and wickedness. (*Secrets of Heaven* §2045)

If we give no thought to the evils within us, that is, if we do not examine ourselves and then refrain from doing them, we wind up inevitably not knowing what evil is and then loving it because of the pleasure it offers us. . . . Anyone who does not know about evil loves it, and anyone who neglects thinking about evil is constantly involved in it. People like this are like blind people, people who cannot see, since thought sees what is good and what is evil the way the eye sees what is beautiful and what is ugly. We are caught up in evil if we consider and intend it and if we think it is hidden from God. . . . If we do then refrain from evil deeds, we do so not because they are sins against God but because we are afraid of the laws and afraid for our reputation. We are still doing them in spirit, though, because it is our spirit that thinks and intends. . . . In the spiritual world where we all arrive after death, no one asks what our faith has been or what our beliefs have been, only what our life has been. . . . The quality of our faith and the quality of our beliefs depend on the quality of our life. . . . Life constructs a belief system for itself and constructs a faith for itself. (*Divine Providence* §101)

What is good is always streaming into us from the Lord, but what is evil in our lives keeps it from being received in the truth we memorize or know. So the more we back away from evil, the more goodness enters into us and adapts to the truth we have. Then religious truth becomes religious goodness in us. We might know truth; we might claim to believe it, spurred on by some worldly goal or other; we might even convince ourselves that it is true. Still, this truth does not come alive as long as we live an evil life. People who act this way are like a tree that has leaves but no fruit. Truth of this type resembles light without any warmth, like the light that shines in winter, when nothing grows. When it does contain warmth, however, it turns into the kind of light that shines in spring, when everything grows. (*Secrets of Heaven* §2388)

How many people . . . live by the Ten Commandments and the Lord's other precepts as a religious practice? How many people . . . are willing to look their own evils in the face and practice actual repentance . . . ? How many devout people practice a repentance that is more than merely verbal and theatrical— confessing that they are sinners and praying (in obedience to the teachings of the church) that God the Father have mercy for the sake of his Son, who suffered on the cross for their sins, took away the damning effect of those sins, and ritually purged them with his own blood? "May the Son forgive our crimes so that we may be presented spotless before the throne of your judgment." Surely everyone can see that this kind of worship is not from the heart; it is only from the lungs. It is external but not internal. We are praying that our sins may be forgiven, yet we are unaware of a single sin within ourselves; and if we are aware of any sin, we either give it our favor and indulgence or else believe that we are purified and absolved of it by our faith without having do any work of our own. By way of comparison, this is like a servant coming in with his face and clothes covered in soot and dung, approaching his master, and saying, "Lord, wash me." Surely his master would tell him, "You foolish servant! What are you saying? Look, there is the water, the soap, and a towel. Don't you have hands? Don't they work? Wash yourself!" (*Survey* §52)

We are to use our own power and do our own work to purify ourselves from sins; we do not stand in impotent faith and wait for God miraculously to wipe them away. (*True Christianity* §71)

When we repent with our lips and not by the way we live, we are not repenting. It is not through repentance of the lips that sin is forgiven but through repentance in one's life. The Lord constantly forgives us our sins, because he is mercy itself. Still, even if we consider our sins forgiven, they cling to us and are not moved aside unless we live by the commandments of faith. The more we live by those commandments, the more our sins are moved aside, and the more they are moved aside, the more they are forgiven. (*Secrets of Heaven* §8393)

Many... [think] that simply believing what the church teaches cleanses us from our evils; some [think that people are cleansed] by doing good... knowing, discussing, and teaching about churchly matters... reading the Word and devotional literature... going to church and listening to sermons and especially taking Communion.... [Still others think they are cleansed by] renouncing the world and being resolutely devout... confessing... sins—the list goes on and on. However, none of these activities cleanses us unless we examine ourselves, see our sins, admit them, accept responsibility for them, and repent by not committing them anymore, doing all this apparently on our own but at heart acknowledging that it comes from the Lord. Until this happens, none of the things I just listed helps. They are being done either for credit or hypocritically. (*Divine Providence* §121)

The moral offenses it is most important for us to give up, escape, and turn away from are adultery, fraud, illicit gain, hatred, revenge, lying, disparaging, [and] arrogance. (*Revelation Explained* §803)

Suppose that in youth and early maturity we have taken into ourselves a pattern of doing something wrong because of the pleasure it gives to our love—cheating, perhaps, or blasphemy, or revenge, or promiscuity. Since we have done so freely, in keeping with our thought, we have made this part of ourselves. Later, though, if we repent, turn away from this behavior, and regard it as sin that is to be rejected, and therefore refrain from it freely and rationally, then we make part of ourselves the good behavior that is opposite to the evil. This good behavior then takes its place in the center and moves the evil toward the periphery, farther and farther out depending on our distaste for and rejection of it. The evil still cannot be ousted to the point of being uprooted, even though it may seem to be so.... This is what happens with all the evil we inherit and with all the evil we act out. (*Divine Providence* §79)

Sins can be taken away from us only by active repentance—that is, by our seeing our sins, begging the Lord for help, and desisting from them. (*The Lord* §17)

Anything good we have thought about or done from the time we were babies right up to the last hour of our life stays with us. So does everything evil; in fact not even the smallest particle of it entirely disappears. All of it remains written in our book of life. In other words, it remains written on [our] memory and on our nature—that is, on our mental and emotional character. This is the material from which we have formed a life and a soul (so to speak) for ourselves, and it remains the same after death. Our virtues never mingle with our faults (nor our faults with our virtues) in such a way that they cannot be untangled, however. If they did mingle in this way, we would be destroyed forever. The Lord provides against it. When we come into the next life, if we have lived a life of loving, charitable goodness, the Lord filters out the evil and uses the good in us to lift us up to heaven. If on the other hand we have lived a life of evil—a life opposed to love and charity—the Lord filters out what is good in us and our wickedness takes us to hell. Such is everyone's lot after death. (*Secrets of Heaven* §2256)

Part Two

THE SOURCE OF LIFE

T HE TOPICS TREATED in Part I, "The Nature of Life"
(freedom, order, use, charity, civil affairs, morality,
marriage and sex, the nature of wisdom, religion, and
evil and sin), all relate primarily to humanity's everyday life rather than to things that look beyond natural existence.

But no theology, no way of life that considers all potential eventualities including possible life after death, can avoid reference to transcendent concepts. Every theology requires metaphysical explanations for the great questions of humanity's origin, nature, and destiny. Although Swedenborg believed that reason and rationality characterized life, he did not imply that all things could be understood merely by the exercise of reason based upon sense impressions. To the contrary, such efforts alone could never lead to wisdom. He said that the ultimate meaning of life could only be understood from revelations given by the divine creator. Consequently, Swedenborg's concept of life contains much that deals with the abstruse. The six topics that follow present the basic aspects of his metaphysics, although a variety of more recondite teachings might easily have been added.

REVELATION

Swedenborg, as has been noted, believed implicitly in two worlds, the natural and the spiritual. He often writes of the connection between the natural and spiritual worlds; the Word of God serves to link heaven and earth. In Swedenborg's view, God has always spoken to human beings and usually has done so in written form to enable them to study and reflect on necessary truths of life. The Swedenborgian view postulates the necessity of God revealing himself to humanity continuously.

The world believes that we can learn many religious principles from nature's light alone, without revelation. These include the principles that there is a God, that we should worship him, that we should love him, and that we will live on after death, as well as many principles resulting from these. Yet . . . without revelation, we are born into the evil that goes with self-love and materialism. Such evil shuts out the influence of the heavens and opens up the influence of the hells, blinding us and casting doubt on the existence of the Deity, heaven and hell, and life after death. This fact is obvious from scholars throughout the globe who have given a higher status to the light of this "nature" of theirs, gained through various branches of knowledge, than to the light enjoyed by others. As everyone knows, they deny the Deity more than others do and acknowledge nature as their deity. When they speak from the heart and not from doctrine, they deny the existence of life after death and of heaven and hell. As a result they deny all the tenets of faith, which they refer to as restraints on the masses. (*Secrets of Heaven* §8944)

If it were not for the Word, no one would have a spiritual understanding. That is, no one would know about God, heaven and hell, and life after death. (*Sacred Scripture* §114)

The Lord is present with us and united to us through the Word because the Lord is the Word and is virtually talking with us in it. There is also the fact that the Lord is divine truth itself, and that is what the Word is. We can see from this that the extent to which we understand the Word determines the extent to which the Lord is present with us and at the same time united to us. This is because our understanding of the Word determines the truth we possess, as well as the faith that arises from that truth. Similarly, our understanding of the Word determines the love we have, as well as the way in which we live, which arises from that love. The Lord is present with us when we read the Word; but he is united to us only when we understand what is true from the Word and only in proportion to that understanding. (*Sacred Scripture* §78)

The main purpose was the Word because the Word is divine truth itself. It teaches us that God exists, that heaven and hell exist, and that there is life after death. It also teaches us how to live and believe, if we want to go to heaven and so be happy forever. Without revelation and therefore (on this planet) without the Word, all of this would have been entirely unknown. (*Secrets of Heaven* §9352)

It was necessary that heavenly truth be available somewhere for people to learn, because we were born for heavenly purposes and should come among heavenly beings when bodily life ends. Religious truth forms the laws of order in the realm where we will be spending eternity. (*Secrets of Heaven* §1775)

People from all over the world have worshiped from various religions. . . . Moreover, religion cannot be imparted except through some kind of revelation, and from there spread from one group of people to another. (*Sketch for "Coda to True Christianity"* §39)

The most ancient people of this world got unmediated revelation, and therefore they did not have a written Word. Later, though, when it was no longer possible to give or receive unmediated revelation without the risk of danger to the spirit, to make sure human communication and union with heaven wouldn't be cut off and die, the Lord decided to reveal divine truth through the Word. (*Draft of "Sacred Scripture"* §27)

The Word has existed at every period, though not the Word we have today. The earliest church, which came before the Flood, had one form. The ancient church, which followed the Flood, had another. In the Jewish religion there is the Word written by Moses and the prophets. And lastly in the new church there is the Word written by the Gospel writers. (*Secrets of Heaven* §2895)

There has been religion from the earliest times and . . . people all over the world have known about God and have known something about life after death. . . . [This knowledge came] later from the Israelite Word. Religious principles spread from these sources into southeast Asia, including its islands; through Egypt and Ethiopia into Africa; and from the coast of Asia Minor into Greece and from there into Italy. But since there was no way the Word could be composed except in the language of representative imagery, in images of things characteristic of this world that corresponded to and therefore signified heavenly realities, the religions of many nations were turned into idolatries—in Greece into fables—and divine attributes and characteristics were turned into individual gods led by one highest God whom people called Jove, from "Jehovah." It is common knowledge that [ancient people] were familiar with paradise, the Flood, sacred fire, and the four ages—from the first Golden Age to the last Iron Age—which serve in the Word to mean the four states of the church. . . . Islam, which came later and wiped out the preceding religious cultures of many nations, was drawn from the Word of both Testaments. (*Sacred Scripture* §117)

Like the earth, we are unable to produce any good unless we have first been sown with religious insights, which enable us to see what to believe and do. The role of the intellect is to hear the Word, while the role of the will is to do it. (*Secrets of Heaven* §44)

People who have religion are people who refrain from desecrating God's name, that is, the holiness of the Word (through contempt, rejection, and any kind of reviling). The way in which people avoid this behavior determines the way they receive religion. Nobody has religion except through revelation, and revelation comes to us through the Word. When people keep themselves from desecrating the holiness of the Word, it must come from their heart, not just from their mouth. If it comes from the heart, they are living from a place of religion, but if it comes from the mouth alone, they are not. In fact, in the latter case, they abstain from desecrating God's name either for their own sake or for the sake of material gain, because the Word serves them as a way to build their reputation and make money. Or, they refrain out of some kind of fear. However, many of them are hypocrites who have no religion at all. (*Revelation Explained* §963)

No one can believe in or love a God whom she or he cannot comprehend under some visible form, so people who acknowledge the incomprehensible [as God] sink into thoughts of the natural creation and consequently believe in no God at all.... It therefore pleased the Lord to be born on [earth] and use the Word to make his birth public. Doing so would not only make it known on this earth but in the process would also reveal it to everyone in the universe arriving in heaven from any planet whatever. For in heaven, everyone communicates with everyone else. (*Secrets of Heaven* §9356)

All of heaven has the Word, and they read and preach from it there just as in the world. Divine truth is the source of angelic intelligence and wisdom, since without the Word no one knows anything about the Lord, about love and faith, about deliverance, or any of the other mysteries of heavenly wisdom. In fact, without the Word there would not be a heaven, just as without the Word there would be no church in the world. If that were the case, we could not be joined with the Lord.... There is no such thing as natural theology without revelation and, in the Christian world, without the Word. If it were not given to us on earth, we would not have it after death either, since the nature of our religion when we are in the world stays the same when we become

spirits after death. On top of that, heaven is not made up of angels who existed before the world, or who were created alongside
the world. Instead, it is made up of angels who used to be people
and were angels inwardly at the time. In heaven, these angels
come into spiritual wisdom (which is inner wisdom) through
the Word, because there, the Word is spiritual. (*Draft of "Sacred
Scripture"* §30)

LIFE AFTER DEATH

*More than perhaps any other seer of history, Swedenborg details a life
after death that consists of real experiences in a world that in many
basic ways is quite similar to the natural world. Angels in heaven do
not have an ethereal or ephemeral existence but enjoy an active life
of service to others. They sleep and wake, love, breathe, eat, talk, read,
work, recreate, and worship. They live a genuine life in a real spiritual
body and world. Swedenborg goes into great detail describing the
three main parts or states of the spiritual world—heaven, hell, and
the world of spirits located between them. This world of spirits serves
as a final preparation ground for a life to eternity in surroundings consistent with the ruling loves of the novitiate. Those whose dominant
loves are good go to heaven, while those who have chosen evil are led
by their perverse loves to hell. There they are kept in external order
and are as happy as their selfish nature permits them to be. They perform uses but, unlike the angels, from compulsion rather than desire.*

The heaven of angels is the reason why everything in the universe
was created, because a heaven of angels is the reason for humankind and humankind is the reason for the heavens we see above

us and the planets they contain.... The heaven of angels . . . looks above all toward what is infinite and eternal, and therefore looks toward multiplying without end, because heaven is where the Divine itself dwells.... Humankind will never come to an end; because if it did, the divine work would come to a halt at a specific quantity and would cease to look toward infinity. (*Last Judgment* §13)

Heaven did not originate in angels who were created angels at the beginning, and . . . hell did not originate in a devil who was created an angel of light and was cast down from heaven. Rather, both heaven and hell are from the human race. Heaven is made up of people who are involved in a love for what is good and a consequent discernment of what is true, and hell of people who are involved in a love for what is evil and a discernment of what is false. (*Divine Providence* §27)

The Lord's divine inflow does not stop in the middle but goes on to its very limit.... There is such a connection and union of heaven with the human race that neither can endure without the other. If the human race were cut off from heaven, it would be like a chain with a link removed, and heaven without the human race would be like a house without a foundation. (*Heaven and Hell* §304)

Hell and heaven are near us and in fact are inside us. Hell is inside a bad person, and heaven is inside a good person. Moreover, whatever hell or heaven we inhabited during our time in the world, that is the hell or heaven we enter after death. (*Secrets of Heaven* §8918)

It can never be said that heaven is outside anyone. It is within.... Unless heaven is within an individual, nothing of the heaven that is outside flows in and is accepted.... People who have lived evil lives and who arrive in heaven bring their souls with them and are tormented like fish out of water, in the air, or like animals in the vacuum in air pumps once the air has been pumped out. (*Heaven and Hell* §54)

Angels and spirits are wholly above or beyond nature. They are in their own world, one that is under a different sun. Further, since spatial intervals are only apparent in that world . . . we cannot say that they are in the ether or in the stars. They are right with us, united to our own spirits in feeling and thought.... The spiritual world is right where we are, not distanced from us in the least. In short, as far as the deeper levels of our minds are concerned we are all in that world, surrounded by angels and spirits there. We think because of the light of that world and love because of its warmth. (*Divine Love and Wisdom* §92)

The general principles of hell are the following three loves: a desire for power based on self-love, a desire to take possession of others' belongings based on a love for the world, and promiscuous desire. The general principles of heaven that are their opposites are the following three loves: a desire for power based on a need to serve, a desire to gain possession of worldly goods based on the need to use them for service, and a true love of marriage. (*Marriage Love* §261)

This is why our spirit, the mind that is in our body, has a complete human form, so that after death we are people just as much as we are in this world. The only difference is that we have cast off the skin that made up our body in this world. (*Divine Providence* §124)

We are in this world to learn heavenly behavior by practicing it here, and that our life in the world is barely like a moment compared to our life after death, which is eternal. [Although] there are not many who believe they will live [again,] ... as soon as we die we are in the other life, ... [and] there we continue our life in the world in every way, and we remain what we had been in the world. I can assert this because ... I have talked with almost everyone I knew during physical life after each has left that life. Doing so has allowed me to learn by personal experience what kind of future awaits us all, and that future is one that matches our life. (*Secrets of Heaven* §5006)

Our first state after death is like our state in this world, since we are then similarly involved in outward concerns. We have similar faces, voices, and character; we lead similar moral and civil lives. This is why it still seems to us as though we were in this world unless we notice things that are out of the ordinary and remember that angels told us we were spirits when we were awakened. So the one life carries on into the other, and death is only a passage. (*Heaven and Hell* §493)

This first state after death lasts a few days for some people, months for some, and a year for some, but rarely more than a year for anyone. (*Heaven and Hell* §498)

Our second state after death is called a state of our deeper interests because then we are given access to the deeper reaches of our minds, or of our intentions and thoughts, while the more outward interests that engaged us in the first state become dormant. (*Heaven and Hell* §499)

When spirits are in this state of their deeper concerns, then it is obvious what kind of people they really were in the world. They actually behave in accord with their own nature. People who were inwardly devoted to the good in the world then behave sanely and wisely, more wisely than when they were living in the world, in fact, because they have been freed from any connection with the body and therefore with the earthly things that darken and cover with a kind of cloud. In contrast, people who were focused on evil in the world then behave foolishly and insanely, more insanely than when they were in the world, in fact, because they are in freedom and are no longer constrained. (*Heaven and Hell* §505)

Our third state after death . . . is one of instruction. This state is for people who are entering heaven and becoming angels. . . . Good people, though, are brought from the second state into a third, which is a state of preparation for heaven by means of instruction. In fact, no one can be prepared for heaven except by knowing at first hand what is good and true, and therefore only by being taught. (*Heaven and Hell* §512)

[This third state is] not for people who are entering hell, because these [people] cannot be taught. As a result, their second state is also their third, and ends in their turning straight toward their own love and therefore toward the hellish community that is engaged in a love like their own. (*Heaven and Hell* §512)

Spirits [have] the power of sensation . . . much keener than they had while living in the body. I know [this] . . . to be true from thousands and thousands of experiences. If you do not want to believe, because of assumptions you make about the spirit, keep it to yourself when you enter the other life. There actual experience will make a believer out of you. Spirits have eyesight, since they live in light, and good spirits, angelic spirits, and angels live in such bright light that the world's noonday light can hardly be compared to it. . . . They also have hearing, and such sensitive hearing that their [former,] physical hearing cannot be measured against it. . . . They have a sense of smell. . . . They have an extremely sensitive sense of touch. . . . They have desires and feelings. . . . They think much more clearly and precisely than they did during the life of the body, packing more into a single mental image than they did into a thousand when they engaged in thought during bodily life. They talk to each other with such great acumen, subtlety, wisdom, and clarity that if we perceived only part of what they said we would be astounded. In short, they have lost absolutely nothing they need in order to be human—and more perfectly human at that—except flesh and bones, and the accompanying imperfections. They acknowledge and perceive that during bodily life the spirit was what actually sensed things. Although sensation seemed to take place in their bodies it was not, in fact, physical. . . . When the body has been laid aside, sensation lives on with much greater acuity and perfection. Life consists in sensation because without it there is no life, and the quality of sensation determines the quality of life. (*Secrets of Heaven* §322)

We are still human beings after we die—so much so that we do not realize we are not still in the physical world. As we used to in the world, we see, hear, and speak. As we used to in the world, we walk, run, and sit. As we used to in the world, we lie down, sleep, and wake up. As we used to in the world, we eat and drink. As we used to in the world, we enjoy making love to our spouse. Briefly put, we are still human in every way.... Death is not the extinction of our life but a continuation of it. (*True Christianity* §792)

In heaven, ... there is no disparity in age, social standing, or wealth. As for age, everyone there is in the flower of youth and remains like that forever. As for social standing, angels see each other in terms of the service they perform. Those who perform a more important service view those who perform a lesser service as peers, and they do not put honors ahead of performing service.... [And] ... the Lord is the Father of them all. Much the same holds true for riches, which in heaven are a dowry consisting of wisdom; and in proportion to the dowry of wisdom they possess, people there are given all the resources they need. (*Marriage Love* §250)

People in heaven are continually progressing toward the springtime of life. The more thousands of years they live, the more pleasant and happy is their springtime. This continues forever, increasing according to the growth and level of their love, thoughtfulness, and faith. As the years pass, elderly women who have died of old age—women who have lived in faith in the Lord, thoughtfulness toward their neighbor, and in contented marriage love with their husbands—come more and more into the flower of growing youth and into a beauty that surpasses any notion of beauty accessible to our sight. Their goodness and thoughtfulness is what gives them their form and gives them its own likeness, making the pleasure and beauty of thoughtfulness radiate from every least corner of their faces so that they become actual forms of thoughtfulness. (*Heaven and Hell* §414)

There are food and drink in heaven just as there are on earth. There are banquets and parties. Leaders there have tables set with the most elegant banquets, with refreshments and delicacies to enliven and restore their spirits. There are entertainments and plays as well, and both instrumental and vocal concerts, all performed to perfection. These give the angels joy.... In the heartfelt desires of all angels there is a hidden current that draws their minds toward some action. This action serves to set their minds at rest and give them a sense of satisfaction; and that satisfaction and calm create a state of mind capable of receiving a desire to be useful from the Lord. Receiving this desire is what constitutes heavenly happiness, which is in turn the life of the joys we have.... In its essence, heavenly food is nothing but love, wisdom, and service combined.... So all in heaven are given food for their bodies depending on the useful service they need to do. (*Marriage Love* §6)

All the people who have been prepared for heaven (this happens in the world of spirits that is halfway between heaven and hell) feel an intense longing for heaven. Soon their eyes are opened and they see a path that leads to some community in heaven. They take this path and go up it, and as they get higher there is a gate with a guard at it. The guard opens the gate so that they go in. Then they are faced with an inspector who tells them on behalf of the manager that they should go farther in and see whether there are any homes there that they can recognize as their own, since there is a new home for every new angel. If they find one they send word back and stay there, but if they do not they go back and say that they have not seen one. They are then examined by a particular wise individual to see whether the light that is in them harmonizes with the light in the community and particularly whether their warmth is in harmony. You see, heaven's light in its essence is divine truth and heaven's warmth in its essence is divine goodness, each radiating from the Lord as heaven's sun. If the light and warmth that are in them are different from the light and warmth of the community—that is, if their truth and goodness are different— they are not accepted. So they leave and follow open paths that connect communities in heaven and do this until they find a community that is in perfect harmony with their own feelings. There they live to eternity, since they are with their own. It is as though they were with their relatives and friends whom they love with all their hearts. . . . Their life is one of utter contentment, suffused with joy because their souls are at peace. There is an indescribable delight in heaven's warmth and light that is imparted to them. That is what it is like for people who become angels. (*Revelation Unveiled* §611)

Heaven comes from the human race, which means that there are angels of both sexes there. . . . By creation itself woman is for man and man for woman, each for the other, and . . . this love is inborn in both sexes. (*Heaven and Hell* §366)

After death, a man is a man and a woman is a woman. . . . These two natures have been so created as to strive toward . . . a union that in fact enables them to become one. . . . Since the tendency to unite is engraved on every detail of the male and the female, then, it follows that this tendency cannot be erased or die when the body dies. (*Marriage Love* §46)

There are marriages in the heavens just as there are on earth. However, the marriages in the heavens are very different from earthly ones. (*Heaven and Hell* §366)

People who have regarded adultery as unspeakable and have lived in chaste love of their marriage are more in the pattern and form of heaven than anyone else. This gives them a total beauty and a constant flower of youth. The pleasures of their love are indescribable, and increase to eternity. (*Heaven and Hell* §489)

The reason separations [of couples married on earth] occur after death is that unions formed on earth are rarely based on any deeper awareness of love. Rather, they are based on a superficial notion of it, which obscures any deeper one. This superficial notion of love originates in or is caused by the sort of concerns that involve worldly or personal desires. Worldly desires have to do primarily with wealth and possessions, while personal desires have to do with rank and position. Then, too, there are various other pleasing qualities that lead people on, like physical beauty and an affectation of good manners. Sometimes even unchaste behavior appeals to people. A further reason for separations is that marriages on earth are contracted within the particular region, city, or town where the partners are born or live, and their choices are strictly limited to the households of acquaintances, and confined still more narrowly to households of similar status. This is why marriages entered into in the world are for the most part outward marriages and not inner ones at the same time; and yet it is the inner union, the union of souls, that makes a real marriage. We cannot be aware of such a union until we shed our outer self and embrace our inner self, which happens after death. This is why separations happen at that time, and afterward new unions take place with partners who are like us, who are compatible with us. Exceptions to this rule are seen when marriages of the latter kind have already been allotted on earth; they are granted to those who from their youth have longed for a proper and loving relationship with only one person, making it their sole choice and seeking it from the Lord. Such people turn away from promiscuity as though it had a bad odor. (*Marriage Love* §49)

A suitable wife is found for the man and a suitable husband for the woman. . . . The only married partners who can be accepted [as a married couple] into heaven on a permanent basis are partners who have been or can be united in a deeper way, or are practically one person. A married pair in heaven is not referred to as two angels but as one. . . . The reason no other married partners are accepted into heaven is that no others are able to live together there—in other words, are able to share the same house, bedroom, and bed. All who are in heaven are connected according to how closely they are aligned in what they love, and this is what determines where they live. In the spiritual world, that is, there is no distance between people, but rather the appearance of distance, and this appearance depends on people's state of life, which in turn depends on the state of their love. This means that people cannot stay for long anywhere but in their own homes, homes provided and assigned according to the nature of their love. If they stay anywhere else, . . . they are short of breath. Two people cannot live in the same house unless they are compatible, and it is particularly the case with married partners that they must be mutually attracted. If they are attracted superficially but not inwardly, then the house or site itself separates them, repels them, and drives them away. . . . Married partners partake of intercourse just as they did in the world, except that they enjoy it more and achieve greater bliss. However, this does not result in reproduction of offspring. Instead, there is a spiritual reproduction, a reproduction of love and wisdom. Married partners partake of intercourse just as they did in the world because after death the male is still male and the female is still female, and an inclination to unite has been implanted in each since creation. In a human being, this is an inclination first of the spirit and then secondarily of the body, so when we become spirits after death that same mutual inclination remains. This inclination necessarily means that there will be the same kind of intercourse. (*Marriage Love* §§50, 51)

I would like to relate some things about the marriages of angels in heaven. They say that their sexual potency is unlimited. After sex they are never tired, let alone sad, but vigorous and cheerful. They spend the night in each other's embrace, as though they were born to be a single person. Their climaxes are long-lasting, and when they try they never fail because lovemaking without climax is like a clogged water pipe—the climax opens it up so it can keep flowing. This creates a connection so that they may be one flesh. The man's vital force combines itself with the woman's vital force and they bond together. They say that the pleasure of their climax cannot be expressed in the words of any language in this world, and cannot even be imagined in anything other than spiritual ideas; even these do not suffice. The angels told me this. (*Revelation Explained* §992 [translation by Brand Erik Odhner])

[Heavenly joy] is the pleasure of doing something that benefits yourselves and others. The pleasure of this kind of service gets its essence from love and its manifestation from wisdom. The pleasure of service that arises from love by means of wisdom is the soul . . . of all heavenly joys. The most delightful gatherings do take place in the heavens, gatherings that bring joy to angels' minds, lift their spirits, warm their hearts, and refresh their bodies. They enjoy these gatherings, though, only after they've made themselves useful in their jobs and pursuits. (*Marriage Love* §5)

All the pleasures of heaven are united to forms of service and dwell within them, because forms of service are the good effects of the love and thoughtfulness that angels are immersed in. Consequently, the nature of each individual's pleasures depends on the nature of that individual's service, and its intensity depends on the intensity of the affection for service. (*Heaven and Hell* §402)

The pleasure afforded by goodness and the charm afforded by truth that make up the bliss in heaven consist not in leisure but in activity. The pleasure and charm of idleness is unpleasant and charmless, but the pleasure and charm of activity lasts, constantly lifts one up, and blesses one. Activity among heaven's inhabitants consists in performing a use (which is the pleasure that goodness affords them) and in developing a wise grasp of truth in order to be useful (which is the charm that truth affords them). (*Secrets of Heaven* §6410)

The opinion of some is that a life of leisure and being waited on by others constitutes heaven. [But] happiness never consists in seeking satisfaction directly from doing nothing. If it did, we would inevitably want to take others' happiness for our own, and if everyone did, no one would be happy. Such a life would not be active but idle, resulting in sluggishness—when as anyone can see life holds no joy unless it is active. Angelic life consists in usefulness and acts of neighborly kindness. Nothing makes angels happier than giving information to spirits newly arrived from the world and teaching them; serving people on earth, making sure that the evil spirits present with them do not go too far, and inspiring them with good; and reviving the dead as they enter eternal life. . . . Angels find more happiness in these activities than could ever be described. In performing them they become images of the Lord. In performing them they love their neighbor more than themselves. This makes heaven. Usefulness (that is, the good that comes of love and charity) is accordingly the substance, the source, and the measure of the angels' happiness. . . . The spirits who thought heavenly joy consisted in relaxing and idly breathing the air of eternal ecstasy were given the opportunity to perceive what such a life would be like. The idea was to embarrass them out of it. They saw that such a life was utterly depressing and that in short order, when inactivity had destroyed all their joy, they would grow sick and tired of it. (*Secrets of Heaven* §454)

There are so many offices and departments in heaven, so many tasks, that there are simply too many to list. There are relatively few in the world. No matter how many people are involved, they are all caught up in a love of their work and tasks out of a love of service—no one out of selfishness or a love of profit. In fact, there is no love of profit for the sake of livelihood, since all the necessities of life are given them for free. They are housed for free, clothed for free, and fed for free. We can see from this that people who have loved themselves and the world more than service have no place in heaven. In fact, our love or affection invariably stays with us after our life in the world. It is not uprooted to eternity. . . . Everyone in heaven is engaged in his or her work according to its correspondence, and the correspondence is not with the work itself but with the use of each particular task. . . . When we are engaged in an activity or a task in heaven that does answer to its use, then we are in a state of life very much like the one we were in in this world. This is because what is spiritual and what is natural act as one by means of their correspondence, but with the difference that [after death] we enjoy a deeper delight because we are engaged in a spiritual life. This is a deeper life, and therefore more open to heavenly blessedness. (*Heaven and Hell* §§393, 394)

Heaven does not consist in altitude but exists wherever people have love and charity (or the Lord's kingdom) inside them, and . . . it does not involve the desire to be superior to others. The wish to be greater than others is not heaven but hell. (*Secrets of Heaven* §450)

In the next life we each receive heaven according to the traits of faith and neighborly love we display, because neighborly love and faith create heaven in us. . . . A life containing heaven is a life incorporating the religious truths and virtues we have learned about. Unless these are the standards and principles of our life, we look for heaven in vain, no matter how we have lived. Without them we are like a reed swaying with every breeze. We bend as readily to evil as to good, because we have no firmly established truth or goodness in us that angels can use for holding us to what is true and good and turning us aside from the falsity and evil that hellish spirits are constantly injecting. (*Secrets of Heaven* §7197)

By its very nature, heaven is full of pleasures, even to the point that if we see it as it really is, it is nothing but bliss and pleasure. This is because the divine good that emanates from the Lord's divine love constitutes heaven both overall and in detail for everyone there; and divine love is the intent that everyone should be saved and should be most profoundly and fully happy. This is why it is all the same whether you say "heaven" or "heavenly joy." Heaven's pleasures are both indescribable and innumerable; but no one can realize or believe anything about their multitude who is wholly wrapped up in pleasures of the body or the flesh. This . . . is because their deeper levels are looking away from heaven toward the world, which is backward. For no one who is wholly involved in pleasures of the body or the flesh (or in love for oneself and the world, which is the same thing) feels any pleasure except in eminence or profit or in physical and sensory gratification. These stifle and smother deeper pleasures of heaven so completely that people do not even believe such pleasures exist. (*Heaven and Hell* §§397–98)

The love of doing good without thought of reward holds a pleasure which itself is an everlasting reward. Every feeling of love is permanently inscribed on a person's life and has heaven and eternal happiness instilled in it by the Lord. (*Secrets of Heaven* §9984)

Heaven is from the human race ..., not only that portion of it born within the church but also the portion born outside it.... This means that heaven includes everyone who has lived a good life since the very beginning of our planet. Anyone familiar with the continents and regions and nations of this world may gather what a multitude of people there are on our whole globe. Anyone who goes into the mathematics of it will discover that ... thousands of people die on any given day ... [and] millions every year; and this has been going on since the earliest times.... All of these people have arrived in the other world ... after their decease, and they are still arriving.... Most of the earliest people [entered heaven], because they thought more deeply and spiritually and were therefore enveloped in heavenly affection; while for later ages it was not so many [entering heaven] because as time passed we became more externally minded and began to think more on the natural level, which meant that we were enveloped in more earthly affection.... The immensity of the Lord's heaven may also be gathered simply from the fact that all children, whether born within or outside the church, are adopted by the Lord and become angels, and their number amounts to a quarter or a fifth of the whole human race. . . . Every child—wherever born, whether within the church or outside it, whether of devout or irreverent parents—is accepted by the Lord at death. Every child is raised in heaven, is taught and is permeated with affections for what is good according to the divine design and thereby with firsthand knowledge of things true, and is then perfected in intelligence and wisdom, so to speak, and admitted into heaven to become an angel. You can gather what a vast multitude of heaven's angels has come. . . . The vastness of the Lord's heaven also follows from the fact that all the planets we can see in our solar system are earths, and especially that there are untold more in the universe, all inhabited. (*Heaven and Hell* §§415, 416, 417)

The whole of heaven presents the image of a single human, called the universal human, to which absolutely everything in a person corresponds. . . . Angels in heaven all appear in human form. Evil spirits in hell look like people to each other too, as a result of their delusions, but in heaven's light they look grotesque. How appalling or horrible the deformity is depends on the evil they adopt. They look like this because evil inherently goes against order, so it goes against the human form. (*Secrets of Heaven* §4839)

Those who are part of the universal human breathe freely when they are exercising a loving goodness. . . . The individuals there are each in their element when they are in their heaven, and come under the influence of heaven as a whole. Everyone there is a focal point for the influence of all and is therefore in perfect balance.... The miraculous form of heaven [is] produced by the Lord alone, so it comes in every variety. (*Secrets of Heaven* §4225)

There are people who love the Lord, show charity to their neighbor, benefit their neighbor from the heart according to the good in her or him, and possess a conscience for what is just and fair.... On the other hand, there are people who love themselves and their worldly advantages, and do good only because of the law, their position, worldly riches, and the status these bring. Deep inside they are ruthless, cherish hatred and vengefulness toward their neighbor out of arrogance and greed, and enjoy seeing their neighbor hurt if she or he does not cater to them.... They are in hell. (*Secrets of Heaven* §4225)

People ... believe that if we only have confidence in our beliefs at the moment of death, we can go to heaven, no matter what our attitude throughout the course of our life.... Anyone can be let into heaven, because the Lord denies heaven to no one, but that if they were admitted they would be able to tell whether they could live there.... Some who had never wavered in this belief were let in, but when they arrived, they started to suffer, because the life there is one of love for the Lord and love for one's neighbor.... In such an environment they could not breathe. Then they started to smell the stench of their own emotions and consequently to experience the tortures of hell. So they rushed off, saying they wanted to be far away, and wondering how something that was hell to them could be heaven.... People who delight in a desire for evil and falsity cannot possibly mingle with those who delight in a desire for goodness and truth. They are opposites, just as heaven and hell are. (*Secrets of Heaven* §3938)

To the extent that we love ourselves and the world and focus on ourselves and the world exclusively, we estrange ourselves from the Divine and move away from heaven. (*Heaven and Hell* §360)

The wicked go through so many stages before being damned and sent to hell. People think we are either damned or saved immediately, without undergoing any process. But the reality is quite different: justice carries the day.... We are not damned until we know with deep conviction that we are committed to evil and that it is impossible for us to be in heaven.... Our evilness is displayed openly to us.... We are also warned to desist from evil, but, when evil rules us so thoroughly that we cannot stop.... Gradually, one step at a time ... we end by being damned and sent to hell. That is what happens when we are left to the wickedness of our life. (*Secrets of Heaven* §7795)

There is a form of government just as much among the evil as among the good, or in hell as in heaven. That is to say, there are higher-ups and people under them, without which society would not cling together. However, hierarchy works in an entirely different way in heaven than in hell. In heaven all are equal; they love each other as sisters and brothers do. Nonetheless, some promote others over themselves, if those others excel in understanding and wisdom. In and of itself, love for what is good and true makes everyone yield almost automatically to people who have more wisdom about goodness and more understanding of truth.

In hell, on the other hand, hierarchy has to do with power and therefore with brutality. Domineering types bully anyone who does not cater to their every whim. Everyone views everyone else as an enemy, though superficially they treat each other as friends for the sake of banding together against violence from outsiders. Such an alliance is like the bond among thieves. Underlings constantly aspire to gain power and often do burst into rebellion. When they do, conditions there are grievous, because savagery and cruelty abound. (*Secrets of Heaven* §7773)

ORIGIN, NATURE, AND PROPER DESTINY OF HUMANITY

Swedenborg has much to say regarding the origin, nature, and proper destiny of humanity. His philosophy of human nature postulates a divinely ordered soul as the essence of each individual human being. Each soul is destined for eternal happiness in heaven. Yet each soul must first exist within an earthly body. This combination of soul and body creates a unique human individual capable of receiving life from God. But the individual is no mere animated puppet. Human beings can exercise their freedom to accept or reject the inflowing life and love from the Creator. If people choose to accept, they will eventually enter eternal happiness in heaven. If they refuse to do so, they are permitted to do what they please and direct themselves toward hell. The soul and body meet in the mind. The mind is the individual person shaped through the formative power of the soul. Influx from God through heaven flows into the soul and from the soul into the mind, which in turn activates the body. To live a good life, according to Swedenborg, an individual should look to the Lord through service of the neighbor as the proper object of useful human pursuits. Such a life of use ends in fulfillment, and such a life, contrary to many religious dogmas, is not difficult to lead. On the other hand, a life of evil centers upon the individual's own desires to the detriment of others. Conscience leads a person to know what is right, but life includes trials that may dull the conscience. All people are prone to error, but each day brings fresh opportunities for the performance of use as long as they live. Human beings can regenerate no matter what their previous life, if they genuinely repent and subordinate their own nature to divine order. Such regeneration turns humanity to its proper destiny—a life of continuing happiness in use to all eternity.

Soul, Mind, and Body

There are three things that constitute every human being, namely, soul, mind, and body.... The one deepest inside is our soul, the one in the middle is our mind, and the outermost is our body. Anything that flows into us from the Lord flows into our inmost level of existence, the soul, comes down from there into our middle level, the mind, and down through that into the last level, which is the body. (*Marriage Love* §101)

The soul does not act through the body in that the soul and the body do not consult and engage in decision making with each other. The soul does not command or request the body to do this or that, or say this or that with its mouth. The body does not call for or petition the soul to give it, or supply it with, something. Everything belonging to the soul belongs to the body, mutually and reciprocally. (*True Christianity* §154)

Soul and body . . . make a single unit together. (*Secrets of Heaven* §2005)

The soul is the inmost part of a person, and therefore a person from head to toe. (*Draft Invitation to the New Church* §13)

[It is] a . . . delusion . . . that the actual living part in us, called the soul, is only a bit of thin air or fire that vanishes when we die, and that it dwells in our heart or brain or some other part of us from which it controls the body like a machine. . . . We have an inner self in every part of our outer self that our eye does not see on its own and our ear does not hear on its own but that both operate under the power of the inner self. (*Secrets of Heaven* §5084)

All of us will be judged according to the quality of our souls, and our soul is our life. That is, it is the love of our intentions; and the love of our intentions depends entirely on our acceptance of the divine truth that emanates from the Lord. (*Revelation Unveiled* §871)

The soul . . . is the human form. . . . It is the innermost form of all forms throughout the body. . . . The soul is the actual person, because it is the innermost person. . . . Its form is fully and perfectly human. It is not life, though. It is the direct recipient of life from God. (*Marriage Love* §315)

Pleasure of the soul comes from the love and wisdom the Lord gives us. . . . Since love is what causes us to accomplish things, and since it does this through wisdom, the seat of both love and wisdom is in what we accomplish; and accomplishment is service. Pleasure of the soul flows from the Lord into our soul and comes down through the higher and lower levels of the mind into all our physical senses. That is where it finds its fulfillment in them. (*Marriage Love* §8)

Anything good we have thought about or done from the time we were babies right up to the last hour of our life stays with us. So does everything evil; in fact not even the smallest particle of it entirely disappears. All of it remains written in our book of life. In other words, it remains written on [our] memory and on our nature. . . . This is the material from which we have formed a life and a soul (so to speak) for ourselves, and it remains the same after death. (*Secrets of Heaven* §2256)

The Nature of the Human Mind

Within each of us, good and evil alike, there are two abilities. One of them makes up our discernment and the other our volition. . . . It is by virtue of these two abilities that we are human. (*Divine Providence* §285)

It is not our face that makes us who we are, or even our words, but rather our intellect and will. . . . We have no intellect at birth and no will either. . . . Our intellect and will form step by step from infancy on. That is how we develop into a person. . . . The intellect is formed by means of truth, and the will, by means of goodness—so much so that our intellect is nothing but a conglomeration of that which can be classified as truth, and our will is nothing but an emotional response to that which is called good. (*Secrets of Heaven* §10298)

We are never born into any truth. . . . We have to learn . . . through hearing and sight. By this path, truth needs to be instilled and planted in our memory. As long as it confines itself to the memory, though, truth is merely knowledge. If it is to permeate us, it has to be called up from there and borne deep within. . . . Unless we are rational, we are not human, so the kind and amount of rationality a person has determines the kind and amount of humanity the person has. We cannot possibly be rational unless we have goodness. The goodness that sets us apart from animals is to love God and love our neighbor. This is the source of all human goodness. Such goodness is what truth needs to be introduced into and unite with, within our rational mind. Truth is introduced and united to goodness when we love God and love our neighbor, because truth then takes up residence in goodness. (*Secrets of Heaven* §3175)

We have an earthly mind and a spiritual mind, the earthly mind below and the spiritual mind above. The earthly mind is our mind for this world and the spiritual mind is our mind for heaven. The earthly mind can be called the animal mind, while the spiritual mind can be called the human mind. We are differentiated from animals by our having a spiritual mind that makes it possible for us to be in heaven while we are in this world. It is also what makes it possible for us to live after death. (*Life* §86)

Differences between Human Beings and Animals

A human is human only by virtue of will and intellect. These faculties distinguish humans from animals. All other characteristics are shared between them. (*Secrets of Heaven* §594)

There are two abilities within us, gifts from the Lord, that distinguish us from animals. One ability is that we can discern what is true and what is good. This ability is called "rationality," and is an ability of our discernment. The other ability is that we can do . . . what is good. This ability is called "freedom," and is an ability of our volition. Because of our rationality, we can think what we want to think, either in favor of God or against God, in favor of our neighbor or against our neighbor. We can also intend and do what we are thinking, or when we see something evil and are afraid of the penalty, can use our freedom to refrain from doing it. It is because of these two abilities that we are human and are distinguished from animals. These two abilities are gifts from the Lord within us. They come from him constantly and are never taken away, for if they were taken away, that would be the end of our humanity. The Lord lives in each of us, in the good and the evil alike, in these two abilities. They are the Lord's dwelling in the human race, which is why everyone, whether good or evil, lives forever. However, the Lord's dwelling within us is more intimate as we . . . open the higher levels [of our mind]. By opening them, we come into consciousness of higher levels of love and wisdom and so come closer to the Lord. It makes sense, then, that as these levels are opened, we are in the Lord and the Lord is in us. (*Divine Love and Wisdom* §240)

The souls of unreasoning animals can look only downward to earthly things and connect only with them. Accordingly they perish when their bodies die. Goals are what demonstrate the nature of human and animal life. We humans can form spiritual and heavenly goals and see, acknowledge, believe, and be affected by them, but the only goals animals can form are earthly ones. So we can enjoy the divine environment of purpose and usefulness that exists in heaven and makes heaven, but the only environment animals can enjoy is that of earth's purposes and functions. (*Secrets of Heaven* §3646)

Certain animals seem prudent and clever, seem to have love relationships with partners, seem to have friendship and something akin to kindness, seem to have honesty and benevolence, language, and morality, like humans do. For example, dogs (from an innate ability, as if from their character) know to be faithful guardians, know from the aura of their owner's emotion what the person's will is. They track their owner from the essence of their footsteps and clothes. They know the area and run through it home, even through winding and dark forests. . . . Sense-oriented people say that dogs too have knowledge, intelligence, and wisdom. (*Revelation Explained* §1198)

No one should think that we are human because we have a human face, a human body, a brain, and all the other organs and limbs. These . . . are the things that die and get put in the grave. No, what makes a person human is the ability to think and will as a human and therefore to receive attributes that are divine. . . . This is what distinguishes us from animals tame and wild. In the other world, the way we received those attributes and made them our own during bodily life determines the kind of human being we become. (*Secrets of Heaven* §4219)

Influx, the Key to Life

We are not life but organs receptive of life . . . from God. (*Soul-Body Interaction* §13)

The facts about the life force in everyone—human, spirit, and angel—are that it flows in from the Lord alone (who is life itself) and permeates all of heaven, and hell too.... The life that flows in, however, is received by each of us according to our disposition. Good people receive goodness and truth as goodness and truth, but evil people receive goodness and truth as evil and falsity, and these even turn into evil and falsity in them. The situation here resembles that of sunlight. The sun pours into every object on earth, but each receives it in accord with its nature. The light takes on beautiful colors in beautiful forms, and ugly colors in ugly forms. This is a secret in the world, but nothing is more familiar in the other life. (*Secrets of Heaven* §2888)

There is a general and a particular influence exerted by the Lord through the spiritual world on recipients of that influence in the natural world.... Animals of every kind live by the code ordained by their nature, so a general influence is exerted on them.... They are born with everything they need. They do not need instruction in order to enter on their role. We human beings, on the other hand, do not live by the code ordained for us or by any law of that code, so a particular influence is exerted on us. That is, we have with us angels and spirits through whom the influence is exerted. If we did not, we would hurl ourselves into every kind of wickedness and quickly plunge headlong into the deepest hell. (*Secrets of Heaven* §5850)

[From this particular inflowing] we, unlike animals, can be lifted up above the physical world. We can think analytically and rationally about civil and moral issues within the material world and also about spiritual and heavenly issues that transcend the material world. We can even be lifted up into wisdom to the point that we see God. (*Divine Love and Wisdom* §66)

Within every one of us here—there is a central or highest level ... where the Lord's divine life flows in first and most intimately. It is from this center that the Lord arranges the other, relatively internal aspects within us that follow in sequence according to the levels of the overall design. This central or highest level can be called the Lord's gateway to the angels or to us, his essential dwelling within us. It is this central or highest level that makes us human and distinguishes us from the lower animals, since they do not have it. This is why we, unlike animals, can be raised up by the Lord toward himself, as far as all the deeper levels of our mind and character are concerned. This is why we can believe in him, be moved by love for him, and therefore see him. It is why we can receive intelligence and wisdom, and talk rationally. It is also why we live forever. (*Heaven and Hell* §39)

Love, the Essence of Life

We are exactly the same as the passion that dominates our life. It distinguishes us from others; it creates our heaven if we are good and our hell if we are bad; it is our very will. Consequently it is the very essence of our life, which cannot be changed after death. (*Secrets of Heaven* §8858)

There are three basic loves of which every human being is composed by creation: love for our neighbor, which is really the desire to be of service; love for the world, which is really the desire to possess wealth; and self-love, which is really the desire to control others. Love for our neighbor, or the desire to be of service, is a spiritual love; love for the world, or the desire to possess wealth, on the other hand, is a desire that focuses on material things; while self-love, or the desire to control others, is a desire that focuses on bodily things. We are truly human when love for our neighbor, or the desire to be of service, constitutes our head; love for the world constitutes our body; and self-love constitutes our feet. If love for the world constitutes our head, we are not human except in a kind of simian way; but if self-love constitutes our head, we are not people standing on our feet but are standing on our hands, head down and bottom up. (*Marriage Love* §269)

Love is the . . . essence of our life and . . . what we think is the consequent . . . expression of our life. This means that the words and deeds that flow from our thinking do not originate in our thinking but flow from our love through our thinking. . . . After death, we are not what we think about, but are rather our inclinations and the kind of thinking they inspire; or more accurately, we are our own particular love and the kind of intelligence it inspires. I have also learned that after death we shed anything that is not in harmony with what we love, and more importantly, we gradually take on the face, tone of voice, way of talking, gestures, and mannerisms belonging to our life's love. This is why the entirety of heaven is arranged according to all the different types of motive that arise from a desire to do good, while the entirety of hell is arranged according to all the different types of motive that arise from a desire to do evil. (*Marriage Love* §36)

The Good Life

Good deeds are everything we do, write, or say (both privately and publicly) that does not come from ourselves, but from the Lord. We do, write, and speak from the Lord when we live according to the rules of our own religion. The laws of our religion are that we should worship the one God, and that we must avoid adultery, theft, murder, and bearing false witness. In addition, we must avoid fraud, illicit gains, hatred, vindictiveness, lying, slander, and many other things. All of these behaviors, described not only in the Ten Commandments but also in every part of the Word, are called moral offenses against God, and atrocities. When we avoid these because they are contrary to the Word and as such contrary to God (and also because they are from hell), we live according to the laws of our religion. The more we live according to religion, the more we are led by the Lord. The more we are led by the Lord, the more our actions are good. We are then led to do good for the sake of good, and to speak truth for the sake of truth—not for our own sake or for the sake of worldly things. Usefulness is then a joy to us, and truth, a delight. We are also taught by the Lord day to day what to do and what to say, as well as what to write and speak out about, because when our evil has been put aside, we are continually under the Lord's supervision. . . . Yet we are not directly led or taught by some kind of pronouncement, or by some kind of perceptible inspiration. Instead we are led by an influx into the joy of our spirit. From that inflowing we gain perception, according to the truth that makes up our understanding. When we act on this, it seems like we are acting from ourselves, yet we acknowledge in our heart that we are doing so from the Lord. (*Revelation Explained* §825)

People recognize that one individual has greater ability than another to understand and perceive what is honorable in private life, fair in public life, and good in spiritual life. The reason some excel is that they raise their minds to heavenly considerations, which draws their thoughts away from the outer senses. People who base their thinking on sensory information alone cannot begin to see what is honorable, fair, and good. As a consequence, they rely on [the judgment of] others and speak at length [on the subject] from rote memory. In their own eyes, this makes them wiser than others. However, people who can lift their thinking above their senses possess a greater ability than others to understand and perceive, as long as they put memorized knowledge in its proper place. The deeper the level from which they view an issue, the more ability they have. (*Secrets of Heaven* §6598)

Some people believe it is hard to lead the heaven-bound life ... because they have heard that we need to renounce the world and give up the desires attributed to the body and the flesh and "live spiritually." All they understand by this is spurning worldly interests, especially concerns for money and prestige, going around in constant devout meditation about God, salvation, and eternal life, devoting their lives to prayer, and reading the Word and religious literature. They think this is renouncing the world and living for the spirit and not for the flesh. ... People who renounce the world and live for the spirit in this fashion take on a mournful life for themselves, a life that is not open to heavenly joy, since our life does remain with us [after death]. No, if we would accept heaven's life, we need ... to live in the world and to participate in its duties and affairs. In this way, we accept a spiritual life by means of our moral and civic life; and there is no other way a spiritual life can be formed within us, no other way our spirits can be prepared for heaven. (*Heaven and Hell* §528)

One person can live like another in outward form. As long as there is an inward acknowledgment of the Deity and an intent to serve our neighbor, we can become rich, dine sumptuously, live and dress as elegantly as befits our station and office, enjoy pleasures and amusement, and meet our worldly obligations for the sake of our position and of our business and of the life of both mind and body. ... It is not as hard to follow the path to heaven as many people believe. The only difficulty is finding the power to resist love for ourselves and love of the world and preventing those loves from taking control, since they are the source of all our evils. (*Heaven and Hell* §359)

Reverent and irreverent people, just and unjust people—good and evil people, that is—may have eminence and wealth. Yet ... irreverent and unjust people ... go to hell while reverent and just people ... go to heaven. ... Eminence and wealth, or rank and money, may be either blessings or curses, and that they are blessings for the good and curses for the evil. ... Both rich people and poor, both the prominent and the ordinary, may be found in heaven and in hell. ... For people in heaven, eminence and wealth were blessings in this world, while for people in hell, they were curses in this world. ... They are blessings for people who do not set their heart on them and curses for people who do. To set one's heart on them is to love oneself in them, and not to set one's heart on them is to love the service they can perform and not oneself in them. (*Divine Providence* §217)

An Evil Life

We have been created in such a way that everything we intend, plan, and do seems to us to be happening within ourselves and therefore is being done by us. If it did not seem this way, we would not be human. We could not receive, retain, and claim as our own any trace of what is good and true, any trace of love and wisdom.... If it were not for this lifelike impression we would have no union with God and therefore no eternal life. On the other hand, if we let this appearance lead us to believe that we intend, plan, and ... do good things autonomously and not from the Lord ... we turn ... good into evil within ourselves, thereby creating a source of evil in us. This was Adam's sin. (*Marriage Love* §444)

The love [all deeds] come from is either heavenly or hellish.... The deeds and works of our ... life are hellish if they come from a hellish love, since whatever we do from this love, which is a love for ourselves and the world, we do from ourselves, and whatever we do from ourselves is intrinsically evil. In fact, seen in our own right, or in terms of what is actually ours, we are nothing but evil. (*Heaven and Hell* §484)

At birth we are the basest living creatures among all the wild animals and beasts. After growing up and coming into our own, we would plunge into atrocities of every kind if various restraints did not stop us—external legal restraints, and restraints we place on ourselves in seeking to grow as influential and rich as possible.

We would not stop until we had overpowered every person in the universe and raked up everyone's wealth. We would spare none but those who submitted to us as lowly slaves. That is what each of us is like. . . . If opportunity and ability presented themselves and the restraints were loosened, we would run just as wild as we could. . . . But the Lord can control the evil and the hell we harbor within. In order to subdue the evil in us . . . the Lord regenerates us and gives us the gift of a new will, which is conscience. Through it, the Lord alone achieves every positive result. (*Secrets of Heaven* §987)

Conscience

Goodness and truth flowing in from the Lord stir [inner] conscience. . . . Private and public justice and fairness . . . stir [outer] conscience. There is also an outermost plane that looks like conscience but is not. It consists in doing what is just and fair for the sake of oneself and the world (that is, for the sake of personal position or reputation . . .). These three planes are the governing force in us. . . . If we have been reborn, he governs us on the inner plane. . . . If we have not been reborn but can be and are (in the other life if not during bodily life), he governs us on the outer plane. . . . All others, including the evil, he governs on the outermost plane, which imitates conscience although it is not. If they were not controlled in this way, they would plunge into all kinds of wickedness and insanity. (*Secrets of Heaven* §4167)

Regenerate people feel joy when they do what conscience bids, and distress when forced to act or think against conscience. With the unregenerate, on the other hand, this is not so. Most do not know what conscience is, much less what obeying conscience or violating it is. They only know how to live by principles that advance their own interests, which gives them joy. Going against these principles creates distress for them. Regenerate people have a new will and a new intellect. The new will and intellect are their conscience. . . . Through [this] the Lord puts neighborly kindness and religious truth to work. People who have not been reborn do not have a will but appetite instead, and are therefore attracted to every kind of evil. They do not have true intellect but shallow logic, and therefore sink into every kind of falsity. Regenerate people have heavenly and spiritual life, but unregenerate people have only bodily and worldly life. (*Secrets of Heaven* §977)

Trials

All trials target the love we feel. The severity of the trial matches the nobility of the love. If love is not the target, there is no trial. To destroy a person's love is to destroy the core of that person's life, since love is life. (*Secrets of Heaven* §1690)

Hardly anyone can see what the battles of spiritual crisis accomplish. They are the means for dissolving and shaking off evil and falsity. They are also the means by which we develop a horror for evil and falsity, and gain not only conscience but strength of conscience; and this is the way we are reborn. (*Secrets of Heaven* §1692)

There are spiritual trials and earthly trials. Spiritual trials test the inner self; earthly trials, the outer. Spiritual trials can happen in either the absence or presence of earthly trials. In earthly trials it is our body, status, affluence—in short, our earthly life—that suffers, as for instance when we experience sickness, misfortune, persecution, unjust punishment, and so on. The distress that then arises is what is meant by earthly trials. These challenges . . . can [not] be called trials, only afflictions. They arise out of wounds sustained by our earthly life, a life of self-love and materialism. Hardened criminals sometimes undergo these vexations, and the degree of pain and distress they feel depends on the degree to which they themselves and their worldly advantages are what they love. . . . Spiritual trials, however, test our inner self and attack our spiritual life. In spiritual trials we do not worry about any loss of earthly life but of faith and charity and consequently of salvation. These struggles are often triggered by earthly struggles, because during them, in sickness or pain or the loss of wealth, prestige, and so on, we might find ourselves thinking about the help the Lord offers. . . . If we do think these thoughts, spiritual trial then combines with earthly trial. (*Secrets of Heaven* §8164)

But spiritual struggles are little known today and are not permitted to the extent that they once were, since people are not under the guidance of religious truth and would consequently succumb. (*Secrets of Heaven* §762)

All trial carries with it some kind of despair. . . . Consolation follows. Anyone who is being tested becomes anxious, and the anxiety causes a state of despair over the outcome. The actual struggle is nothing else. Those who are sure of victory feel no anxiety, so they face no test. (*Secrets of Heaven* §1787)

We . . . do not undergo such a test until we reach adulthood. (*Secrets of Heaven* §4248)

While we are being tested, we are essentially starving for goodness and dying of thirst for truth, so when we come out the other side, we eat up goodness like a person starved for food and lap up truth like a person parched for drink. . . . Brightness and good cheer emerge after the murk and anxiety of tribulation. (*Secrets of Heaven* §6829)

Regeneration

It is the constant effort of the Lord's divine providence to unite us to himself and himself to us, and that this union is what we call reformation and regeneration. I explained also that this is the source of our salvation. Can anyone fail to see that union with the Lord is eternal life and salvation? Everyone can see this who believes that we were originally created in the image and likeness of God . . . and who knows what the image and likeness of God are. (*Divine Providence* §123)

People . . . imagine we can be reborn without being tested. Some suppose we can become reborn after undergoing a single crisis. It needs to be known, though, that no one is reborn without trials and that the trials come one after another. . . . Rebirth takes place in order to kill off the life of the old self and instill new, heavenly life. Struggle, then, is clearly inevitable. The life of the old self resists, not wanting to be snuffed out, and the life of the new self can enter only where the life of the old self has been snuffed out. So it is plain that both sides fight, and fight hard, since they are fighting for their life. These varieties of evil cannot all be conquered at one and the same time. They hang on tenaciously, because they took root in our forebears for many ages back, are therefore born into us, and are reinforced by the evil we have actually committed on our own since childhood. All this evil is diametrically opposed to the heavenly goodness that needs to be instilled in us and to become the substance of our new life. (*Secrets of Heaven* §8403)

Trial is the beginning of regeneration. The whole process of rebirth exists in order for us to receive new life. (*Secrets of Heaven* §848)

We are born into every type of evil and consequently into every type of falsity, so on our own we are condemned to hell. In order to be rescued from hell, then, we . . . must be born again, to the Lord as our parent. This rebirth is what is called regeneration. To be reborn, we must start by learning truth. People who are part of the church must learn it from the Word, that is, from teachings gleaned from the Word. The Word and teachings from it teach us what truth and goodness are, and truth and goodness teach us what falsity and evil are. Unless we know all this, we cannot possibly regenerate, because we persist in our vices and therefore in false thinking, calling our vices virtues and our false thinking true. . . . A knowledge of truth and goodness must come first and enlighten our intellect. The reason an intellect has been given to us, you see, is to be illuminated by concepts of goodness and truth, so that these concepts can be embraced by our will and turned into goodness. Truth does not turn into goodness until we will it and willingly act on it. . . . It does not matter whether you describe it as willing what is good or loving what is good, because what we love is what we will. Nor does it matter whether you describe it as understanding the truth that comes of goodness or believing it. So it follows that love and faith form a single unit in a person reborn. This union, or this marriage, is what is called the church, heaven, the Lord's kingdom, and even (in the highest sense) the Lord with humankind. (*Secrets of Heaven* §10367)

As we are formed, our intelligence and wisdom is perfected, and we become human. This is because a person is not human on account of their worldly mind, since our worldly minds make us more like animals. We actually become human through intelligence and wisdom given by the Lord. A person is beautiful to the angels of heaven to the degree that they are intelligent and wise. In as much as they reject, suffocate, and twist the goodness and truth from the Word . . . (and so refuse intelligence and wisdom) they are monsters and not humans, because these are the qualities of the devil. (*Revelation Explained* §790)

According to God's laws, he can forgive us our sins only to the extent that we follow our laws and stop doing them. God cannot regenerate us spiritually beyond the point to which we, following our laws, have regenerated ourselves in an earthly way. God makes an unceasing effort to regenerate us and save us, but he cannot do it unless we prepare ourselves as a vessel, leveling a pathway for God . . . and opening the door. (*True Christianity* §73)

When we are being reborn, we are not stripped of delight in the lowly pleasures belonging to the body and to the lower mind. No, we enjoy these pleasures fully after rebirth, even more fully than before, but in inverse proportion. Before rebirth, enjoyment of the lower pleasures was our entire life, whereas after rebirth, the good we do out of neighborly love is our entire life. Enjoyment of the lower pleasures then serves as an intermediate plane and ultimate foundation on which spiritual goodness with all its happiness and bliss can rest. (*Secrets of Heaven* §8413)

We have no right at all to say we have regenerated until we acknowledge and believe that charity is the most important part of our faith and until we feel love for our fellow humans and show mercy to them. (*Secrets of Heaven* §989)

Until we have been reborn, we cannot help thinking about a reward. When we have been reborn, things change. Then we chafe if anyone thinks we are helping our neighbor for the sake of a reward, because what makes us feel pleased and blessed is helping, not being repaid. (*Secrets of Heaven* §8002)

In regenerate people, the inner self is in charge and the outer self obeys. In people who have not been reborn, the outer self is in charge, while the inner self retires and seems to disappear. Regenerate people recognize what the inner self is and what the outer self is. . . . People who are not regenerate have no idea at all what the inner and outer self are. They cannot tell even if they think about it, because they have no idea what the goodness and truth of a faith based on kindness is. . . . The regenerate person . . . and . . . the unregenerate one . . . are as different as summer and winter, or light and darkness. So the regenerate person is a living individual, while the unregenerate one is a dead individual. (*Secrets of Heaven* §977)

Before rebirth we live by the commandments of faith, but afterward we live by the commandments of charity. Before rebirth none of us knows about charity from experiencing it, only from learning about it.... After rebirth, though, we know what charity is from experiencing it, because we then love our neighbor and wish our neighbor well with all our heart. We also live then by a law internalized by us, because we act under the influence of neighborly love. This state is radically different from the previous one. People in the first state are in the dark regarding religious truth and goodness, but people in the latter state have relative clarity. (*Secrets of Heaven* §8013)

When we are regenerated, the whole pattern of our life is inverted. We become spiritual instead of earthly.... we act out of thoughtfulness and make the elements of that thoughtfulness part of our faith. Still, we are spiritual only to the extent that we are attentive to what is true, since everyone is regenerated by means of truths and through living by them. It is truths that enable us to know what life is, and life that enables us to practice truths. This is how goodness and truth are united in the spiritual marriage where we find heaven. (*Divine Providence* §83)

We have no idea how we are reborn and scarcely even *that* we are. If you do want to know, just look at what your goals and intentions are, which you likely do not reveal to anyone. If you aim at something good, if you care more about your neighbor and the Lord than yourself, you are at some stage of rebirth. If you aim at something bad, if you care more about yourself than your neighbor or the Lord, be aware that you are not at any stage of rebirth. (*Secrets of Heaven* §3570)

The time it takes to regenerate is not fixed . . . in such a way that we can say, "Now I have finished." The states of evil and falsity that each of us has inside are beyond counting. They exist not only as individual states but also as multilayered composites and need to be dispelled to the point where they no longer appear. . . . In some of our states we can be described as more perfect, but in countless others we cannot. In the other life, those who were reborn during bodily life and who lived lives of faith in the Lord and charity toward their neighbor are constantly being perfected. (*Secrets of Heaven* §894)

Whenever some specific passion leads us, no matter what direction it goes, if we follow it, we consider it a liberating thing. But it is devilish spirits—whose company we keep and whose stampede we join—that sweep us along. This we consider the epitome of freedom. In fact we believe life would become positively miserable and even end if we were deprived of such a condition. It is not merely that we know of no other kind of life; we also receive the impression that no one can make it into heaven except through misfortune, poverty, and renunciation of pleasure. But this is untrue. . . . We never come into a free condition until we have regenerated and until the Lord leads us by means of a love for what is good and true. Once we arrive there, we are able to see and perceive for the first time what liberty is, because we then realize what life is and what true pleasure in life and happiness are. Up to that time, we do not even know what goodness is, and occasionally we refer to the height of evil as the greatest good. (*Secrets of Heaven* §892)

Our rebirth in this world is only a foundation for the perfection of our life to eternity. (*Secrets of Heaven* §9334)

Proper Destiny of Humanity

We are not born to live for ourselves alone; we are born to live for others.... The goal is to be in a state in which we can serve our fellow citizens, our community, our country, the church, and therefore the Lord. People who pursue this goal are providing well for themselves to eternity. (*True Christianity* §406)

There are four phases to our lives. We pass through them as we go from infancy to old age. The first phase is when our behavior follows other people's instructions. The second is when our behavior is our own, and our intellect restrains us. The third is when our will pushes our intellect and our intellect restrains our will. The fourth is when our behavior is deliberate and purposeful. These phases of our lives are phases of the life of our spirit, however; they do not necessarily relate to our body. Our body can behave morally and speak rationally, and yet our spirit can intend and think things that are the opposite of morality and rationality. It is clear from pretenders, flatterers, liars, and hypocrites that this is the nature of our earthly self. Clearly, people like this have a dual mind—their mind can be divided into two parts that do not agree. It is different for people who have benevolent intentions and think rational thoughts, and as a result do good things and speak rationally. (*True Christianity* §443)

To serve the Lord by acting on his commandments—that is, by obeying them—is to be free, not enslaved, because our truest freedom consists in being led by the Lord. . . . He breathes goodness directly into our will, and although our actions come from him when they are based on that goodness, they feel as though they come from us, so they feel free. Everyone who lives in the Lord enjoys this freedom, which brings with it indescribable happiness. (*Secrets of Heaven* §8988)

The Lord loves everyone and wants what is best for everyone. What is best for us means what is of service to us; and because the Lord provides what is best, or what is of service, indirectly through angels, and in the world through individuals, he gives those who serve faithfully a desire to serve and the reward for that desire, which is an inner bliss. This is eternal happiness. (*Marriage Love* §7)

No individual enjoys any desire or perception so much like someone else's as to be identical, and no one can to eternity. Further, desires can bear fruit endlessly and perceptions can multiply endlessly: . . . we can never exhaust the store of knowledge. (*Divine Providence* §57)

We can be perfected in knowledge, intelligence, and wisdom to eternity. (*Marriage Love* §134)

When we are granted truth we are perfected in understanding and wisdom, and when we are perfected in understanding and wisdom we are blessed with happiness forever. (*Secrets of Heaven* §5651)

THE NATURE OF THE UNIVERSE

In Swedenborg's view, the spiritual and natural worlds form two interrelated parts of one creation. The two result from the outflowing of divinely creative love and wisdom. They are so interdependent that one cannot survive without the other. Creation looks to one end—a heaven peopled with spiritual beings who first established their eternal individuality in the natural world. All earths have the same essential purpose, and, therefore, endless varieties of the human race exist. On any one globe, everything material serves the uses of humanity in order that a person in her or his turn may better perform uses to other people. Such human service truly promotes the divine purpose in the universe.

There is a spiritual world and a natural world.... The spiritual world is where angels and spirits live, and the natural world is where people live.... Earthly objects represent spiritual attributes and correspond to them.... The earthly dimension cannot possibly come into existence except as a result of some cause prior to it. Its cause lies on the spiritual plane. No earthly object exists that does not trace its cause to that plane. Physical forms are the effect and cannot appear as causes, still less as causes of the causes, or first origins. Instead, they take a shape that suits the use they will serve in the place where they exist.... Everything in the earthly realm represents that facet of the spiritual realm to which it corresponds. (*Secrets of Heaven* §§2990, 2991)

Each and every item in the world presents some image of the Lord's kingdom and so of heavenly and spiritual attributes. (*Secrets of Heaven* §1409)

God is absolute love and absolute wisdom. His love includes an infinite number of feelings. His wisdom includes an infinite number of perceptions. The correspondences of those feelings and perceptions are all the things that appear on earth. This is where the birds and animals come from. This is where the trees and shrubs come from. This is where the grains and crops come from. This is where the plants and grasses come from. God is not extended but he is everywhere in what is extended. He is in the universe from beginning to end. Because he is omnipresent, correspondences of the qualities of his love and wisdom are found everywhere in the physical world. In . . . the spiritual world, there are similar correspondences surrounding those who receive feelings and perceptions from God. . . . In [the spiritual] world God creates things of this kind in a moment to match the feelings of angels, while in [the physical] world things like this were originally created in a similar way but there was a provision for their perennial renewal from generation to generation; and so creation goes on. The reason why there is instantaneous creation in [the spiritual] world while in [the physical world] there is a creation that continues across generations is that the atmospheres and soils in [the former] are spiritual while those in [the latter] are physical. Physical things were created to cover spiritual things the way animal or human skin covers the body, inner and outer bark cover tree trunks and branches, membranes and meninges cover brains, sheaths cover nerves, coatings cover nerve fibers, and so on. (*True Christianity* §78)

The created universe is actually a coherent work, from love by means of wisdom. (*Soul-Body Interaction* §5)

Everything in the world was created in the image of something in heaven. Elements of the earthly realm grow out of elements in the spiritual realm the same way effects grow out of their causes. That is why . . . all of nature is a theater representing the Lord's kingdom. (*Secrets of Heaven* §8812)

Inner and outer things are not arranged in a continuum, though, but with definite boundaries. There are two kinds of levels, continuous and noncontinuous. Continuous levels are like decreasing levels of light from a flame, all the way to darkness, or like decreasing amounts of sight from objects in the light to objects in the shade, or like levels of density of the atmosphere from the lowest to the highest. . . . Noncontinuous or distinct levels, though, are separated like prior and posterior, cause and effect, producer and product. . . . There are these kinds of stages of production and composition in everything in the world. (*Heaven and Hell* §38)

What exists on a deeper plane is more perfect than that which exists on a shallower plane, and the two share no similarity except through correspondence. (*Secrets of Heaven* §10181)

The universe, from beginning to end and from first to last, is so full of divine love and wisdom that you could call it divine love and wisdom in an image. . . . Every single thing that comes to light in the created universe has such an equivalence with every single thing in us that you could call us a kind of universe as well. There is a correspondence of our affective side and its consequent thought with everything in the animal kingdom, a correspondence of our volitional side and its consequent discernment with everything in the plant kingdom, and a correspondence of our outermost life with everything in the mineral kingdom.... We find in [the spiritual] world all the things that occur in the three kingdoms of our physical world, and they reflect the feelings and thoughts. (*Divine Love and Wisdom* §52)

Before creation, God was love itself and wisdom itself. That love and that wisdom had a drive to be useful. Without usefulness, love and wisdom are only fleeting abstract entities, and they do indeed fly away if they do not move in the direction of usefulness. The two prior things without the third [love and wisdom without usefulness] are like birds flying across a great ocean that eventually become worn out, fall into the ocean, and drown. God created the universe so that usefulness could exist. Therefore the universe could be called a theater of useful functions.... We, the human race, are the principal reason for creation.... All aspects of the divine design have been brought together and concentrated in us so that God can perform the highest forms of useful service through us. Without usefulness as a third party, love and wisdom would be as unreal as the heat and light of the sun would be if they had no effect on people, animals, and plants. That heat and that light become real by flowing into things and having an effect on them. (*True Christianity* §67)

Creation began from the highest or inmost things because it began from the Divine, and it proceeded to the last or outermost thing.... (The outermost level of creation is the physical world, including our globe of lands and seas and everything on it.) Once all this was finished, then humanity was created, and into humanity was gathered every level of the divine design from first to last. (*Last Judgment* §9)

The physical world [receives] from the spiritual world, and the spiritual world [receives] from Divinity. (*Divine Love and Wisdom* §293)

There are other planets with people living on them. . . . Such large bodies as the wandering stars—some of them bigger than ours—are not empty masses, created just to parade around the sun and shine for one earth. They ought to have a nobler function than that. The human race is the breeding ground for heaven, and if you believe (as everyone should) that the sole purpose for which the Deity created the universe was the emergence of a human race, and from it, heaven, you must believe there are people wherever there is a planet. . . . They are bodies made of earthly stuff, since they reflect [rather than generate] sunlight. They circle the sun just as our own planet does and consequently create years for themselves, and the seasons of spring, summer, fall, and winter (with differences, depending on climate). They also rotate on their axes as our planet does and consequently create days for themselves, and the times of day: morning, noon, evening, and night. (*Secrets of Heaven* §6697)

Everything in the universe, great and small, has been created by God. That is why the universe and absolutely everything in it is called "the work of Jehovah's hands" in the Word. People do say that the whole world was created out of nothing, and they like to think of "nothing" as absolutely nothing. However, nothing comes from "absolutely nothing" and nothing can. This is an abiding truth. This means that the universe, being an image of God and therefore full of God, could be created by God only in God. God is reality itself, and everything that exists must come from that reality. To speak of creating something that exists from a "nothing" that does not exist is a plain contradiction of terms. Still, what is created by God in God is not a continuation of him, since God is intrinsic reality and there is no trace of intrinsic reality in anything created. If there were any intrinsic reality in a created being, it would be a continuation of God, and any continuation of God is God. (*Divine Love and Wisdom* §55)

There are two suns by means of which the Lord created everything, the sun of the spiritual world and the sun of the physical world. . . . The reason the Lord created the universe and everything in it by means of the spiritual world's sun is that this sun is the first emanation of divine love and wisdom, and . . . everything comes from divine love and wisdom. There are three components of everything that has been created, no matter how large or how small it is: a purpose, a means, and a result. There is nothing created that lacks these three components. (*Divine Love and Wisdom* §§153, 154)

This spiritual universe could not exist, however, without a physical universe in which it could accomplish its useful effects. Therefore at the same time a sun was created as the source of all things physical. Through this sun by means of its heat and light . . . atmospheres were created. . . . Through these atmospheres the globe of lands and seas was created. Here people, animals, and fish, and trees, bushes, and plants were created out of earthly materials consisting of soils, stones, and minerals. This is only a very general sketch of creation and its stages. The particular and individual stages could not be explained without filling volumes of books. They would all come to the following conclusion, though: that God did not create the universe out of nothing. . . . Nothing is made out of nothing. God created the universe through the sun in the angelic heaven—a sun that comes from his underlying reality and is therefore pure love together with wisdom. The universe, meaning both worlds (the spiritual and the physical), was created out of divine love through divine wisdom, as every single thing in it witnesses and attests. (*True Christianity* §76)

The purpose of all elements of creation . . . is an eternal union of the Creator with the created universe. This does not happen unless there are subjects in which his divinity can be at home. . . . We are those subjects, people who can raise themselves and unite with apparent autonomy. . . . Through this union, the Lord is present in every work he has created. (*Divine Love and Wisdom* §170)

Everything in creation was intended for humanity's use, benefit, and enjoyment, either directly or indirectly. Since these things were created for us, it follows that they were also created for serving the Lord, who is the life within us. (*Draft on Divine Wisdom* §12)

This world is a complex structure of useful functions arranged and prioritized for the sake of the human race, the source of the angelic heaven. . . . Among the marvels of this world is that the lowly insects called silkworms clothe with silk and magnificently adorn both women and men from queens and kings down to maids and butlers. And the lowly insects called bees supply wax for the lamps that give churches and royal courts their splendor. (*True Christianity* §13)

Everything in the universe is procreated and formed in conformity with usefulness, in the performance of a useful service, and to accomplish a useful service. (*Marriage Love* §183)

It is humankind through which the natural world is united to the spiritual world, [and] we are the means of the union. For there is within us a natural world and also a spiritual world . . . so to the extent that we are spiritual, we are a means of union. However, to the extent that we are natural and not spiritual, we are not a means of union. (*Heaven and Hell* §112)

People who do not know the mysteries of heaven may believe that angels exist apart from us and that we exist apart from angels, but . . . no angel or spirit exists apart from humankind and . . . no human being exists apart from angels and spirits. I can testify also that the way we are joined together is mutual and reciprocal. . . . Humankind and the heaven of angels make up a single whole and depend on each other mutually and reciprocally for their existence, which means that neither can be parted from the other. (*Last Judgment* §9)

Almost all who come into the next life from the world think that hell is the same for everyone and heaven is the same for everyone, when in reality there are unlimited differences and variations in either case. Hell is never exactly the same for one person as for another, nor is heaven—just as there is never one person, spirit, or angel who is exactly the same as another. . . . All unity is formed out of harmony among many. . . . The way that the many harmonize determines what kind of unity they have. . . . So every community in the heavens forms a single unit, as do all the communities—or the whole of heaven—taken together. The Lord alone makes this happen, and he does so through love. (*Secrets of Heaven* §457)

In the entire created universe, no two things can possibly be the same. . . . Neither can the world have two identical situations over time. . . . This is also provable from human faces. In the whole world, not one face exists that is the same as another or similar in every way. Nor will there ever be two identical faces to eternity. Infinite variety like this could occur only as the result of God the Creator's infinity. (*True Christianity* §32)

DIVINE PROVIDENCE

The subject of divine influence in human affairs has been debated by philosophers and theologians through the centuries. Swedenborg, in keeping with the explicit character of his writings, goes to considerable length to spell out the details of the workings of divine providence. For him, providence works in every general and particular happening. All events, no matter how minute, contribute to the eternal welfare of humanity. But since an individual would feel her- or himself to be nothing if they perceived the workings of providence in advance, the Lord provides that humanity not see these workings "in the face" but merely sense them "in the back" after time has gone by. If people live a prudent life yet do not place confidence in their own prudence, they will merge themselves with the stream of providence. An individual's life, while it will be marked by the normal ebb and flow of human events, will generally be directed well. Still they are free to direct themselves otherwise, for the laws of providence provide always for humanity's continual freedom. In Swedenborg's view of life, an all-wise providence looks constantly to allowing each individual the power to seek her or his own happiness.

The working of divine providence for our salvation starts with our birth and lasts to the end of our life and then on to eternity. . . . A heaven from the human race is the purpose of the creation of the universe and . . . in its working and progress this purpose is the divine provision for our salvation. . . . All the things outside us, all the things that are useful to us, are secondary purposes of creation. . . . If these [material things] constantly function according to the laws of the divine design established at the very beginning of creation, then surely the primary purpose of creation, the salvation of the human race, must constantly function according to its laws, which are the laws of divine providence. Just look at a fruit tree. See how it is first born from a tiny seed as a delicate sprout, how this gradually develops into a trunk that sends out branches, how these are covered with leaves, and how it then produces flowers, bears fruit, and sets new seeds in the fruit that provide for its endless future. It is the same for all shrubs and all the meadow grasses. Every least thing involved in this process is constantly and wonderfully moving from its purpose to its goal according to the laws of its design. Why should the primary purpose, a heaven from the human race, be any different? Can there be anything in its process that is not going on at every instant in accord with the laws of divine providence? Since there is this relationship between our life and the growth of a tree, we may draw a parallel or comparison. (*Divine Providence* §332)

Divine omnipotence exists within the divine design and follows that design in its governing called providence. Constantly and to eternity divine omnipotence acts in accordance with the laws of its own design. God cannot act against them or change even the tip of one letter of them, because he *is* the divine design along with all its laws. (*True Christianity* §73)

Divine providence is the divine design as it relates specifically to our salvation. Further, just as there is no design without its laws (the laws actually define it) and every law is a design because its source is the design . . . as God is the design, he is also the law of his design. We must then say the same of his divine providence, that just as the Lord is his providence, he is also the law of his providence. . . . The Lord cannot act contrary to the laws of his divine providence, because to do so would be to act contrary to himself. Further, there is no such thing as doing something unless it affects some subject and does so through some means. . . . We are the subject of divine providence; its means are the divine truths that provide us with wisdom and the divine generosity that provides us with love. It is through these means that divine providence accomplishes its purpose, which is our salvation. . . . The working of divine providence for our salvation starts with our birth and lasts to the end of our life and then on to eternity. (*Divine Providence* §331)

Unless the Lord led us at every moment, even the very smallest, we would wander from the way of reformation and die. Every shift and change in the state of our minds shifts and changes a whole series of present and therefore of subsequent events. . . . It is like an arrow shot from a bow. If the arrow were deflected the least bit from its aim at the target, the deflection would be huge at a distance of a mile or more. That is how it would be if the Lord were not guiding the states of our minds at every least moment. The Lord does this in keeping with the laws of his divine providence, including the law that says it seems as though we are leading ourselves. However, the Lord foresees how we will lead ourselves and constantly makes adjustments. (*Divine Providence* §202)

The Lord's divine providence is all-inclusive because it deals with details and . . . deals with details because it is all-inclusive. The reason the Lord acts from the center and the boundaries at the same time is that this is the only way the whole and all its elements can be kept connected. The things in between depend in sequence on the central ones, all the way to the boundaries, and they are all gathered together at the boundaries; . . . there is a gathering at the boundaries of everything that comes from the First. (*Divine Providence* §124)

[The Lord] alone governs the pattern, not only in general, as people assume, but even in the smallest details. The smallest details, after all, are what make up the general whole. To speak of a general whole and remove the particulars from it would be exactly the same as speaking of a sum without parts. It would be speaking of a something that contains nothing. As a result, it is absolutely wrong . . . to suggest that the Lord's providence is universal and not specific in the most minute way. To provide and govern in general and not in the smallest particulars is to provide for and govern exactly nothing. This is a philosophical truth, but amazing to say, philosophers themselves—even the loftier ones—do not think or conceive of providence this way. (*Secrets of Heaven* §1919)

If the Lord's providence did not concern itself with the smallest details, we could never be saved or even stay alive, because life is from the Lord, and every moment of life has a series of consequences reaching to eternity. (*Secrets of Heaven* §6490)

Divine foresight and providence clearly covers the very smallest details, then. If it did not, or if it took only a general sort of care, the human race would perish. (*Secrets of Heaven* §5122)

The Lord sees and foresees absolutely everything, and provides for and arranges absolutely everything. Sometimes he does so with bare tolerance, sometimes with reluctant permission, sometimes with acceptance, sometimes with pleasure, and sometimes with a will. (*Secrets of Heaven* §1755)

Divine providence differs from all other guidance and watchful care in this, that providence constantly looks to eternity and constantly leads to salvation. The means to this end are varying states both cheerful and grim that we cannot possibly comprehend, although all of them contribute to our eternal life. (*Secrets of Heaven* §8560)

When the Lord is with someone, he leads that person and provides that every event, whether sad or happy, turns to that person's benefit. That is what divine providence is. (*Secrets of Heaven* §6303)

Divine providence is so undercover in its operation that we barely even see a trace of it, and yet it is active in the most minute details of our life in this world, from infancy through old age, and then afterward to eternity. Divine providence takes eternity into consideration even in every tiny detail. Since divine wisdom in itself is none other than the end goal, providence acts from the goal, within the goal, and toward the goal. The final goal is that we become wisdom and love, and so become a dwelling place for, and an image of, divine life. (*Revelation Explained* §1135)

The constant objective of divine providence is to unite what is good to what is true and what is true to what is good within us. This is how we are united to the Lord. (*Divine Providence* §21)

The Lord's divine providence is constantly working to unite what is true with what is good and what is good with what is true within us, because this union is the church and heaven. This union exists in the Lord and in everything that emanates from him. It is because of this union that heaven is called "a marriage," as is the church; so in the Word the kingdom of God is compared to a marriage. (*Divine Providence* §21)

It is a law of divine providence that we should act in freedom in accord with reason. (*Divine Providence* §71)

The Lord leads us each by our inclinations, bending us by his silent providence, because he guides us in freedom. (*Secrets of Heaven* §4364)

It is a law of divine providence that we should not sense or feel anything of the working of divine providence, but that we should still know about it and acknowledge it. (*Divine Providence* §175)

The Lord in his divine providence is constantly leading us in our freedom, and to us it seems as though this freedom were our own. Leading us against ourselves in freedom is like lifting a massive and stubborn weight from the ground with jacks and not being able to feel the weight and the resistance because of their strength. Or it is like people surrounded by enemies intent on murder, unaware that a friend is leading them out by unknown paths and will later disclose the plan of their enemies. (*Divine Providence* §211)

[The Lord] . . . foresaw that nothing good would ever take root in us unless we were free, since what takes root when we are not free dissolves as soon as evil approaches or we are tested. This the Lord foresaw, and the fact that on our own, in our freedom, we would head for the deepest hell. So he provides that if we do not let ourselves be led freely to heaven, he will divert us to a milder hell, but that if we allow ourselves to be led freely toward goodness, he will take us to heaven. This shows what foresight and providence are, and that what is foreseen is provided for. . . . Every split second of our life carries with it a series of consequences that continues forever. Each moment is like a new starting point for another series. . . . Since the Lord foresaw from eternity what we would be like now and forever, his providence must obviously be present in the smallest facets, governing us and (again) bending us in this direction by continually moderating our freedom. (*Secrets of Heaven* §3854)

We would go counter to God and deny him if we were to see clearly what divine providence itself is doing [because] we are caught up in the pleasure of our love, and this pleasure is integral to our very life. . . . If we were to sense, then, that we were constantly being led away from our pleasure, we would be as angry as though someone were trying to destroy our life and would regard that person as our enemy. To prevent this from happening, the Lord does not show himself clearly in his divine providence. Rather, he uses it to lead us subtly, the way a hidden stream or favorable current carries a boat. (*Divine Providence* §186)

We are allowed to see divine providence from behind but not face to face, and when we are in a spiritual state, not in a materialistic state. Seeing divine providence from behind but not face to face is seeing it after the fact but not before; and seeing it when we are in a spiritual state and not in a materialistic state is seeing it from heaven and not from this world. (*Divine Providence* §187)

It is a law of divine providence that we should not be compelled by outside forces to think and intend and so to believe and love in matters of our religion, but that we should guide ourselves and sometimes compel ourselves. (*Divine Providence* §129)

No one is reformed by miracles and signs. . . . [Nor are they] reformed by visions or by conversations with the dead, because they compel. (*Divine Providence* §§130, 134)

If we sensed and felt the working of divine providence, we would not act freely and rationally, and nothing would seem to be really ours. The same would hold true if we knew what was going to happen. . . . We would have no sense of self and therefore no sense of worth, and without this it would make no difference whether we did evil or good, whether we had faith in God or accepted the principles of hell—in short, we would not be human. . . . If our immediate feelings and sensations told us that we were being led, we would not be aware of our own life. We would then be impelled to make sounds and motions almost like some statue. If we were aware of our life, the only way we could be led would be like someone in handcuffs and shackles or like a cart horse. Can anyone fail to see that in this case we would have no freedom, and that if we had no freedom we would have no rationality? That is, we all think because we are free and we all think freely; and anything we think apart from this freedom or in any other way does not seem to be ours but to come from someone else. No, if you look into this more deeply, you will find that we would have no thought, let alone rationality, and that therefore we would not be human. . . . If we knew the result or the outcome because of some divine prediction, our reason would yield, and our love would yield along with it. . . . The very delight of our reason is to see a result that comes from love by thought, not as it happens but beforehand, or not in the present but in the future. This is what gives us what we call *hope*, waxing and waning in our rationality as we see or await a result. This delight finds its fulfillment in the outcome, but then both it and thought about it are cancelled. The same thing would happen if an outcome were foreknown. The human mind is constantly engaged with three matters called purposes, means, and results. If any of these is lacking, our mind is not engaged in its own life. The impulse of our volition is the originating purpose; the thinking of our discernment is the effectual means; and the action of the body, the speech of the mouth, or our physical sensation, is the result of the purpose that is achieved through thought.... The human mind is not engaged in its life when it is occupied only with the impulse of its volition and nothing more, and ... the same is true if it is occupied only with the result. This means that our minds do not have their life from any one of these elements by itself, but from the three of them together. This life of our minds wanes and ebbs when an outcome is foretold. (*Divine Providence* §§176, 178)

Since foreknowledge of what will happen destroys our essential human nature, our ability to act in freedom and rationally, no one is allowed to know the future. We can, though, draw conclusions about the future on the basis of reason. This is what brings reason and all its powers to life. This is why we do not know what our lot will be after death or know anything that is happening before we are involved in it, because if we did know we would no longer think in our deeper self about what we should do or how we should live in order to reach some particular goal. We would only think with our outer self that this was coming; and this state closes the deeper levels of the mind where, principally, those two abilities of our life dwell, freedom and rationality. (*Divine Providence* §179)

None of this could happen if it did not seem to us that we think autonomously and manage our lives autonomously. I have already given ample evidence that we would not be human if it did not seem to us that we lived on our own and that we therefore thought, intended, spoke, and acted on our own. It follows from this that unless we seemed to be managing everything that has to do with our occupations and our lives by our own prudence, we could not be led and managed by divine providence. It would be as though we stood there with our hands hanging limp, mouths open, eyes closed, holding our breath and waiting for something to flow into us. In this way we would divest ourselves of everything human, which we get from the sense and feeling that we live, think, intend, speak, and act on our own. (*Divine Providence* §210)

All strength, prudence, understanding, and wisdom come from the Lord. (*Secrets of Heaven* §2694)

[The] subject [of divine providence] is barely accessible to any human mind, and least of all to the minds of those who trust in their own shrewdness. Such people take credit for anything that turns out well for them. All other events they ascribe to luck or chance. Few of them attribute anything to divine providence. So they see happenstance as due to dead rather than living causes. (*Secrets of Heaven* §8717)

In relation to divine providence . . . our own prudence is like that dust in relation to the entire atmosphere; it is nothing by comparison, and what is more, it falls down. People who ascribe everything to their own prudence . . . are like wanderers in shadowy forests who do not know the way out. (*Secrets of Heaven* §6485)

Goodness from the Lord is present in people who love the Lord more than anything and love their neighbor as themselves. Goodness from a merely human source is present in people who love themselves more than anything and despise their neighbor in comparison with themselves. The latter are also the people who have care for the morrow, because they rely on themselves, while the former are those who do not have care for the morrow, because they rely on the Lord, as discussed [in] §8478 [see below]. People who rely on the Lord are constantly receiving good from him, because whatever happens to them, whether it looks favorable or unfavorable, is still good, because it contributes as a means to their eternal happiness. People who rely on themselves, however, are constantly bringing evil down on themselves, because whatever happens to them, even if it looks favorable and fortunate, is still evil and so contributes as a means to their eternal misfortunes. (*Secrets of Heaven* §8480)

Anyone who goes with the flow of providence is constantly being carried to a happy destination, no matter what the appearance is along the way. People who trust the Deity and give him all the credit are the ones who are in the flow of providence. People who trust themselves alone and take all the credit for themselves are the ones who are not in the flow of providence. They oppose providence, because they strip it from the Deity and claim it for themselves. Be aware too that the more we go with the flow of providence, the more at peace we are. Then again, the more at peace we are because of a religiously inspired goodness, the more we are under divine providence. People of this type are the only ones who see and believe that the Lord's divine providence is involved in everything large and small, including even the very smallest details of all . . . and that divine providence looks to eternity. People who are opposed to providence, though, are barely willing even to use the Word. Instead they ascribe everything to human prudence, and if not to prudence, then to luck or chance. Some ascribe everything to fate, which they trace back not to the Deity but to the material world. Anyone who does not attribute everything to herself or himself or else to the material world they label naive. (*Secrets of Heaven* §8478)

The Divine

In Swedenborg's view of life, the power of the Divine permeates every aspect of human existence. Preceding selections chosen for this presentation of the teachings of Swedenborg clearly show that no subject, from the simple to the most abstract, can be presented without reference to the omnipotence, omniscience, and omnipresence of God. The passages that follow deal with some of the more difficult aspects of the concept of the Divine. Philosophers and theologians have often disagreed on such topics as the virgin birth, the glorification, the Trinity, and the nature of God's influx into the lives of human beings. Swedenborg avoids none of these difficult subjects and says, moreover, that proper understanding of the Divine must accompany individual and collective human progress. Religious leaders sometimes refer to these and related subjects as "mysteries of faith." The decline of religious conviction in the twentieth-century world of science was doubtless partly due to hesitancy and confusion surrounding these mysteries of faith.

Yet as Emerson once said, "The Religion that is afraid of science dishonours God and commits suicide." [29] *Swedenborg would agree. The entire spread of his theological teachings supports his contention that God's new revelation permits all who so desire to enter intellectually into the mysteries of faith. On no subject is this more evident than in Swedenborg's commentaries on the Divine.*

In the created universe there is nothing living except the Divine-Human One—the Lord—alone, . . . nothing moves except by life from God, and . . . nothing exists except by means of the sun from God. So it is true that in God we live and move and have our being. (*Divine Love and Wisdom* §301)

The first step in religion is the concept that God exists and is to be worshiped. The first fact that needs to be known about the nature of God is that he created the universe and that the created universe depends on him for its existence. (*Secrets of Heaven* §6879)

A right concept of God . . . is the very core of the thinking of anyone who has a religion. All the elements of religion and of worship focus on God; and since God is involved in every element of religion and worship, whether general or particular, unless there is a right concept of God there can be no communication with heaven. This is why every nation is allotted its place in the spiritual world according to its concept of a human God. This [understanding of God as human] is where the concept of the Lord is to be found, and nowhere else. We can see very clearly that our state after death depends on our avowed concept of God if we consider the opposite, namely that the denial of God, and in the Christian world, a denial of the Lord's divinity, constitutes hell. (*Divine Love and Wisdom* §13)

Inwardly . . . the idea of God is central to everything having to do with the church, religious practice, and worship. Theological concepts dwell at a higher level in the human mind than all other concepts, and the highest theological concept is the idea of God. Therefore if our idea of God is false, everything else that follows from it derives a falseness from or becomes falsified by the source from which it originates. Whatever is highest (which is also what is inmost) acts as the essence of the things that result from it. (*Survey* §40)

Only God is substance in and of itself and is therefore essential being. . . . There is no other source of the arising of things. Many people do see this, since reason enables them to. However, they do not dare argue it for fear that they might arrive at the thought that the created universe is God because it is from God—either that, or the thought that nature is self-generated, which would mean that its own core is what we call "God." As a result, even though many people have seen that the only source of the arising of everything is God and God's essential being, they have not dared move beyond the first suggestion of this. If they did, their minds might get ensnared in a so-called Gordian knot with no possibility of escape. The reason they could not disentangle their minds is that they were thinking about God and God's creation of the universe in temporal and spatial terms, terms proper to the physical world, and no one can understand

God and the creation of the universe by starting from the physical world. Anyone whose mind enjoys some inner light, though, can understand the physical world and its creation by starting from God, because God is not in time and space. . . . Even though God did create the universe and everything in it out of himself, still there is not the slightest thing in the created universe that is God. (*Divine Love and Wisdom* §283)

God is everywhere, within us and outside us. (*Divine Love and Wisdom* §130)

There is an inflow from God into us. . . . From [this] divine inflow into human souls . . . , it follows that in everyone there is an inner voice saying that God exists and that there is one God. (*True Christianity* §§8, 9)

God's eternity is not an eternity of time. Since there was no time before the world came about, I realized that it was completely pointless to ponder such questions about God. Furthermore, since the Divine "from eternity," that is, the Divine independent of time, did not involve days, years, and centuries—they were all an instant for God—I concluded that God did not create the world in a preexisting context of time; time was first introduced by God as part of creation. (*True Christianity* §31)

God is in all time without being bound by time and in all space without being bound by space. Nature, on the other hand, is in all time and bound by time, and in all space and bound by space. . . . Nature comes from God and not from eternity. It is within time . . . [and] space [is] intrinsic to it. (*Marriage Love* §328)

Thinking about one God opens heaven to people, because there is only one God. On the other hand, thinking about multiple gods closes heaven up, since the idea of multiple gods destroys the idea of one God. Thinking about the true God opens heaven, because heaven and everything about it come from the true God. On the other hand, thinking about a false God closes heaven, since no god except the true God is acknowledged in heaven. Thinking about God the Creator, Redeemer, and Illuminator opens heaven, since this trinity constitutes the true God. Thinking about the infinite, eternal, uncreated, all-powerful, all-present, and all-knowing God opens heaven as well, because these are the attributes of the one true God's essence. On the other hand, thinking about a living person as God, a dead person as God, or an idol as God closes up heaven because none of these are all-knowing, all-present, all-powerful, uncreated, eternal, or infinite. They were not the source of creation and redemption, and they do not illuminate anything. (*Revelation Explained* §1097)

Those who worship one God in whom there is a divine trinity and who is therefore one person become more and more alive, and become angels on earth. Those, however, who convince themselves to believe in a plurality of gods because there is a plurality of divine persons become more and more like a statue with movable joints, inside which stands Satan, talking through its hinged mouth. (*True Christianity* §23)

In the Lord is the trinity of divinity itself, divine humanity, and their divinely holy influence, and the three are one. (*Secrets of Heaven* §3061)

This Trinity did not exist before the world was created. It developed after the world was created, when God became flesh. It came into existence in the Lord God the Redeemer and Savior Jesus Christ. Nowadays the Christian church asserts that the divine Trinity came into existence before the world was created: Before time, Jehovah God bore a Son. Then the Holy Spirit went out from them both. Each of the three is a God all by himself, in that each is a single self-sufficient person. Because this concept does not square with any type of reasoning, it is called a mystery. The only way to grasp the concept is to think that the three share one divine essence—an essential eternity, immensity, and omnipotence and therefore equal divinity, glory, and majesty.... Such a concept becomes a trinity of gods and is therefore not a divine Trinity. (*True Christianity* §170)

The apostolic church knew no trinity of persons.... Eventually, however, people started to [confuse the Trinity].... [This] crime...was committed by Arius and his followers. Therefore Constantine the Great called a council in Nicaea, a city in Bithynia. The people who had been called there to throw out Arius's damaging heresy invented, defended, and gave sanction to the idea that three divine persons—the Father, the Son, and the Holy Spirit—had existed from eternity, each with a personality, a reality, and a continued existence of his own. They also concluded that the second person, the Son, came down, took on a human manifestation, and brought about redemption; and that his human nature was divine because of a hypostatic union. Through this union he had a close relationship with God the Father. From that time on, balls of atrocious heresies relating to

God and the person of Christ began to roll out across the globe, raising the head of the Antichrist, dividing God into three and the Lord the Savior into two, and destroying the temple that the Lord had erected through his apostles to the point where not one stone was left attached to another. (*True Christianity* §174)

Those who took part in the Council of Nicaea that gave birth to this posthumous child called the Athanasian Creed had no other concept of the Trinity except a trinity of gods, as any can see who merely keep their eyes open as they read it. Since then they have not been the only people thinking in terms of a trinity of gods; the Christian world thinks in terms of no other Trinity because its whole concept of God comes from that creed and everyone now lives in a faith based on those words. I submit it as a challenge to everyone—both laity and clergy, laureled professors and doctors as well as consecrated bishops and archbishops, even cardinals robed in scarlet and in fact the Roman pope himself— that the Christian world nowadays thinks of no other Trinity except a trinity of gods. You should all examine yourselves and then speak on the basis of the images in your mind. The words of this creed—the universally accepted teaching about God—make it as clear and obvious as water in a crystal bowl. For example, the creed says that there are three persons, each of whom is God and Lord. It also says that because of Christian *truth,* people ought to confess or acknowledge that each person is individually God and Lord, but that the catholic or Christian *religion* . . . forbids us to say three gods or lords. This would mean that truth and religion, or truth and faith, are not the same thing; they are at odds with each other. The writers of the creed added the point that there is one God and Lord, not three gods and lords, so that they would not be exposed to ridicule before the whole world. Who would not laugh at three gods? On the other hand, though, anyone can see the contradiction in the phrase they added. (*True Christianity* §172)

All who go to the other world from the Christian religion these days think of the Lord the same way they think of any other person. They picture the Lord as being not only separate from divinity . . . also separate from Jehovah and in addition separate from his holy influence. They do talk of one God, but they think three and actually divide the Deity in three. They split it into persons, calling each one God and assigning a distinct role to each. As a result, Christians are said in the other world to worship three Gods, because they think three, even if they say one. (*Secrets of Heaven* §5256)

When told that the Father, the Son, and the Holy Spirit are the three essential components of the one God as our soul, our body, and our actions [are the essential components of a human being], the human mind may still think that three persons play the roles of these three essential components. . . . When, however, we see the Father's divinity as the soul, the Son's divinity as the body, and the Holy Spirit's divinity (or divinity emanating) as action, and we see them as three essential components of one single God, then they become understandable. For the Father has his own divinity; the Son derives his divinity from the Father; and the Holy Spirit derives its divinity from them both.

Since they share the same soul and essence, they constitute one God. . . . We are all capable of using the trinity within each of us to picture the Trinity in the Lord. In every one of us there is a soul, a body, and our actions. It is the same in the Lord. . . . There is a divine trinity in the Lord and a human one in us. (*True Christianity* §§168, 169)

The same three essential components—soul, body, and action—existed and still exist in the Lord God the Savior, as everyone acknowledges. . . . The Lord's soul came from Jehovah the Father. . . . The Son whom Mary bore is the body of that divine soul; for what develops in the mother's womb is the body that was conceived by and derived from the soul. . . . Actions make a third essential component because they come from both the soul and the body; for things produced have the same essence as the things that produce them. The three essential components that are Father, Son, and Holy Spirit are one in the Lord as our soul, our body, and our actions [are one in us]. (*True Christianity* §167)

Two things—love and wisdom—constitute the essence of God; but three things constitute the essence of God's love: his loving others who are outside of himself, his wanting to be one with them, and his blessing them from himself. The same three constitute the essence of his wisdom because in God love and wisdom are united. . . . It is love that wants those three things, however, and wisdom that brings them about. (*True Christianity* §43)

The Lord uses the truth emanating from himself to govern all things, down to the most minute. He governs not the way a monarch does in the world but the way God does in heaven and the universe. A monarch in the world has only the most general oversight; his lieutenants and functionaries oversee the particulars. It is very different with God, who sees everything, knows everything from eternity, provides everything to eternity, and holds everything in order.... The Lord ... has oversight not only of the entire whole but also of the particulars.... The Lord manages the universe both directly through divine truth from himself and indirectly through heaven. (*Secrets of Heaven* §8717)

What flows in from the Lord is a goodness born of heavenly love and therefore of love for one's neighbor. In this love the Lord is present, because he loves the whole human race and wants to save every member of it forever. Since the goodness born of this love comes from him, he is in such goodness, so he is present in a person who possesses it. (*Secrets of Heaven* §6495)

Everything that emanates from the Lord instantly permeates the universe ... and since it progresses by degrees through an unbroken series of intermediate stages, it passes not only into animals but even beyond them into plants and minerals. (*Marriage Love* §397)

The Lord is constantly present with every human being, the evil as well as the good. No one would be alive if the Lord were not present. Only when we let him in, however—that is, believe in him and do what he commands—does he come in. The Lord's constant presence is what makes us rational, and what gives us the capacity to become spiritual. (*True Christianity* §774)

Our salvation is the Lord's constant working with us from earliest infancy all the way to the end of life, and ... this is entirely divine, in no way possible for any mere human. Its divine quality makes it at once a matter of omnipresence, omniscience, and omnipotence; . . . from beginning to end . . . our reformation and regeneration and therefore our salvation is all a matter of the Lord's divine providence. (*Revelation Unveiled* §798)

The Lord alone is to be worshiped. If you do not fully understand worship of the Lord, you may believe that he loves to be worshiped and desires to receive glory from us in the same way we might give others what they ask in order to win recognition for ourselves. People who believe this have no idea what love is, let alone what divine love is. Divine love is to desire worship and glory not for the sake of the Divine but rather for the sake of us and our salvation. When we worship the Lord and give glory to him, we are being humble. When we are humble, our sense of autonomy subsides, and the more it subsides, the more we accept what is divine. Our sense of autonomy is all that stands in the way of what is divine, because it consists of evil and falsity. That is what the glory of the Lord is, and it is the ultimate reason for worship of him. To seek glory for one's own sake is a result of self-love, and heavenly love is as different from self-love as heaven is from hell. Divine love differs infinitely more. (*Secrets of Heaven* §10646)

Outward worship is described as corresponding to inward when it contains the essential ingredient, which is heartfelt reverence for the Lord. Such reverence is not possible in the least except where charity, or love for one's neighbor, exists. Charity, or love for our neighbor, contains the Lord's presence. With it, we can adore the Lord from the heart. When we have charity, our reverence comes from the Lord, since the Lord gives us all the ability to revere him and all the vital essence of our veneration. It follows, then, that the kind of charity we have determines the quality of our adoration, that is, the quality of our worship. All worship is veneration, because it has to have reverence for the Lord within it in order to be worshipful. (*Secrets of Heaven* §1150)

Our belief in God and union with him depend on our living a good life. Everyone who knows anything religious can know about God. People can talk about God from this knowledge or from memory, and some of them can even think intelligently about God. If they do not live good lives, though, this brings only a presence. They are still perfectly capable of turning away from him and turning toward hell, which they do if they live evil lives. Heartfelt belief in God, though, is possible only for people who live good lives. Depending on those good lives, the Lord turns them away from hell and toward himself. (*Divine Providence* §326)

The more closely we are united to the Lord, the wiser we become. . . . The more closely we are united to the Lord, the happier we become. . . . The more closely we are united to the Lord, the more clearly we seem to have our own identity, and yet the more obvious it is to us that we belong to the Lord. (*Divine Providence* §§34, 37, 42)

When we are being led by the devil, we are helpful for the sake of ourselves and the world, but when we are being led by the Lord, we are being helpful for the sake of the Lord and heaven. All the people whose helpfulness comes from the Lord are people who are abstaining from evils as sins, while all the people whose helpfulness comes from the devil are people who are not abstaining from evils as sins. Evil comes from the devil, but service, or doing good, comes from the Lord. This is the only way to tell the difference. They look alike outwardly, but their inward form is completely different. One is like a golden object that has slag inside, while the other is like a golden object that is pure gold all the way through. One is like a piece of artificial fruit that looks outwardly like fruit from a tree but actually is colored wax with powder or tar inside, while the other is like fine fruit, appealingly delicious and fragrant, with its seeds within. (*Divine Providence* §215)

We cannot see God except from the qualities we have inside us. If, for instance, we harbor hatred, we view God from the standpoint of hatred. If we are merciless, we see him as merciless. If on the contrary we possess love for our neighbor and show mercy, we view him from the standpoint of these qualities and consequently see him in them. (*Secrets of Heaven* §8819)

When people acknowledge that their entire life comes from the Lord, he gives them the delight and blessedness of his love, to the extent that they acknowledge him, and to the extent that they prioritize usefulness. This happens when people, as if on their own, give over their whole life to the Lord via recognition of and belief in him originating in love. In turn, the Lord gives over the goodness of his life to them, which comes along with every kind of joy and blessing. On top of that, he allows them to sense it and feel it in themselves, deeply and exquisitely, as if it were their own. This happens in proportion to how deeply they desire at heart what they know through faith. Therefore, the feeling is mutual—we are grateful to the Lord that he is in us and that we are in him, and the Lord is glad for us that we are in him and that he is in us. This is the joining of the Lord with us and of us with the Lord through love. (*Revelation Explained* §1138)

THE TWO ADVENTS

Few today, even among practicing Christians, find it easy to accept the idea that God came on earth in the person of Christ. Moreover, the virgin birth of Jesus has been a major religious hurdle for nonbelievers, most of whom reject the idea out of hand. Swedenborg believed that Christ indeed was God on earth. He further states that only such a divine advent could have restrained the then-rising power of evil in the world. Therefore, Swedenborgian theology rests upon acceptance of the central tenet of Christianity. But the most unusual aspect of his view centers in Swedenborg's quiet assurance that he was used as the means by which God revealed himself to humanity a second time. Unlike the first advent, which required God's personal presence, the second coming could be made through the human mind of Swedenborg. By the eighteenth century, the human race had evolved to the point where a rational explanation of divine revelation was both possible and necessary. This claim has doubtless been the chief obstacle to a wider acceptance of Swedenborg's theology. The somewhat questioning faith of the nineteenth century gave way to the widespread skepticism of the twentieth century. In such a climate, the Swedenborgian concept of two divine advents evokes scant support. Yet Swedenborg's sincere belief in his startling claim can scarcely be questioned, and the testimony of those who have studied Swedenborg, whether they became converts to his faith or not, indicates that his writings cannot be lightly dismissed. Further understanding of his second-advent claim expands the meaning that Swedenborg has given to the divine nature of the coming of Jesus.

Jehovah God ... came down and took on a human manifestation for the purpose of forcing everything in heaven, everything in hell, and everything in the church back into the divine design. The power of hell had become stronger than the power of heaven, and on earth the power of evil had become stronger than the power of goodness; therefore total damnation stood threatening at the door. By means of his human manifestation, which was divine truth, Jehovah God lifted this pending damnation and redeemed both people and angels. ... If the Lord had not come into the world no one could have been saved. (*True Christianity* §3)

The reason why the hells had risen so high was that by the time the Lord came into the world the whole planet had completely alienated itself from God by worshiping idols and practicing sorcery; and the church that had existed among the children of Israel and later among the Jews had been utterly destroyed by their falsifying and contaminating the Word. After death both of the above groups arrived in the world of spirits. Over time they grew in numbers there to such an extent that they could not have been driven out thereafter if God himself had not come down and used the power of his divine arm to deal with them. (*True Christianity* §121)

The human race had wholly corrupted itself by its evil life and resulting distorted convictions. People's lower levels started to rule their upper levels; their earthly dimension started to rule their spiritual dimension. In fact Jehovah (the Lord) could no longer flow into them through the universal human, or heaven, and restore those elements to order. So the Lord had to come in order to take on a human dimension and make it divine. By this means he would restore order, so that all of heaven would relate to him as the only human and correspond to him alone. (*Secrets of Heaven* §3637)

Around the time of the Lord's Coming, hellish spirits occupied much of heaven. By coming into the world and making the human nature in himself divine, the Lord drove them out and threw them down into the hells. In this way he liberated heaven from them and gave it as an inheritance to people belonging to his spiritual kingdom. (*Secrets of Heaven* §6306)

Had the Lord not come into the world and opened up the Word's inner depths, communication with the heavens through the Word would have been broken off, and once it was broken, the human race on this planet would have died out. We are unable to think anything true or do anything good . . . except . . . through heaven from the Lord. The Word . . . opens heaven. (*Secrets of Heaven* §10276)

People generally believe that the Father sent his Son to suffer cruel hardships, including even death on the cross, and that when he observed the Son's suffering and worthiness, he therefore took pity on the human race. Anyone can see, however, that Jehovah did not become merciful as a result of observing his Son, because he is mercy itself. The secret to the Lord's Coming into the world is that in himself he was to unite divinity with humanity, and humanity with divinity, which could be accomplished only through the heaviest of trials. So as a result of this union, salvation would be able to come within the grasp of the human race, which no longer possessed any trace of heavenly, spiritual, or even earthly goodness. (*Secrets of Heaven* §2854)

Jehovah God could not have taken these actions and made them effective without a human manifestation. . . . An invisible person cannot shake hands or talk with a visible one. In fact, angels and spirits cannot shake hands or talk with us even when they are standing right next to our bodies or in front of our faces. No one's soul can talk, or do things, with anyone else except through its own body. The sun cannot convey its light and heat into any human, animal, or tree, unless it first enters the air and acts through that. It cannot convey its light and heat to any fish unless it passes through the water. It has to act through the element the entity is in. None of us could scale a fish with a knife or pluck a raven's feathers if we had no fingers. We cannot go to the bottom of a deep lake without a diving bell. In a word, one thing needs to be adapted to another before the two can communicate and work with or against each other. Suffering on the cross was the final trial the Lord underwent as the greatest prophet. It was a means of glorifying his human nature, that is, of uniting that nature to his Father's divine nature. It was not redemption. There are two things for which the Lord came into the world and through which he saved people and angels: redemption, and the glorification of his human aspect. These two things are distinct from each other, but they become one in contributing to salvation.... *Redemption* was ... battling the hells, gaining control over them, and then restructuring the heavens. *Glorification,* however, was the uniting of the Lord's human nature with the divine nature of his Father. This process occurred in successive stages and was completed by the suffering on the cross. All of us have to do our part and move closer to God. The closer we come to God, the more God enters us, which is his part. It is similar with a house of worship: first it has to be built by human hands; then it has to be dedicated; and finally prayers are said for God to be present and unite himself to the church that gathers there. The union itself [between the Lord's divine and human natures] was completed by the suffering on the cross, because this suffering was the final spiritual test that the Lord went through in the world. Spiritual tests lead to a partnership [with God]. During our spiritual tests, we are apparently left completely alone, although in fact we are not alone—at those times God is most intimately present at our deepest level giving us support. Because of that inner presence, when any of us have success in a spiritual test we form a partnership with God at the deepest level. In the Lord's case, he was then united to God, his Father, at the deepest level. (*True Christianity* §§125–26)

It was not the Lord's divine nature that suffered, it was his human nature; and then the deepest union, a complete union, took place.... Redemption and the suffering on the cross must be seen as separate. Otherwise the human mind gets wrecked as a ship does on sandbars or rocks, causing the loss of the ship, the helmsman, the captain, and the sailors. It goes astray in everything having to do with salvation by the Lord. If we lack separate ideas of these two things we are in a kind of dream; we see images that are unreal and we make conjectures based on them that we think are real but are just made up.... Although redemption and the suffering on the cross are two different things, nevertheless they become one in contributing to salvation. When the Lord became united to his Father, which happened through the suffering on the cross, he became the Redeemer forever. (*True Christianity* §§126, 127)

There is a belief that the Lord in his human manifestation not only was but still is the Son of Mary. This is a blunder, though, on the part of the Christian world. It is true that he was the Son of Mary; it is not true that he still is. As the Lord carried out the acts of redemption, he put off the human nature from his mother and put on a human nature from his Father. This is how it came about that the Lord's human nature is divine and that in him God is human and a human is God. (*True Christianity* §102)

Anyone might be astonished to hear that the Lord had evil inside him inherited from his mother, but... one human being could never be born to another without inheriting evil from him or her. But the evil we inherit from our father and the evil we inherit from our mother are very different. The evil we inherit from our father lies deep within and remains forever, because it can never be rooted out. This was not true of the Lord, because he was the son of his Father Jehovah and was therefore divine or Jehovah on the inside. The evil we inherit from our mother, conversely, belongs to our outer self. This evil was present in the Lord. . . . The fact that he underwent spiritual trials provides clear evidence that he inherited evil from his mother. No one who is free of evil can ever be tempted; it is the evil in us that is the source and means of our trials. The Lord *was* tested and underwent trials so severe that no one could ever endure even a millionth of what he went through. (*Secrets of Heaven* §1573)

In short, the Lord was attacked by all the hells from early in his youth up to the very end of his life in the world, while he was continually routing, subduing, and vanquishing them. This he did purely out of love for the entire human race. Since his love was not human but divine, and the greater the love the harder the struggle, you can see how fierce his battles were and how savage on the part of the hells. (*Secrets of Heaven* §1690)

The Lord glorified his human nature—that is, he united it with the divine nature of the Father (with the divine nature that was within him from conception, that is). This was to the end that the human race might be united to God the Father in him and through him. (*Revelation Unveiled* §618)

The Lord had two states while he was in the world: one called being emptied out; the other called glorification. The prior state, being emptied out, is described in many passages in the Word, especially in the Psalms of David, but also in the Prophets. There is even one passage in Isaiah 53 where it says, "He emptied out his soul even to death" (Isaiah 53:12). This same state also entailed the Lord's being humbled before the Father. In this state he prayed to the Father. In this state he says that he is doing the Father's will and attributes everything he has done and said to the Father. The following passages show that he prayed to the Father: Matthew 26:36–44; Mark 1:35; 6:46; 14:32–39; Luke 5:16; 6:12; 22:41–44; John 17:9, 15, 20. The following show that he did the Father's will: John 4:34; 5:30. The following show that he attributed everything he had done and said to the Father: John 8:26, 27, 28; 12:49, 50; 14:10. In fact, he cried out on the cross, "My God, my God, why have you abandoned me?" (Matthew 27:46; Mark 15:34). Furthermore, without this state it would have been impossible to crucify him. The state of being glorified is also a state of union. The Lord was in this state when he was transfigured before three of his disciples. He was in it when he performed miracles. He was in it as often as he said that the Father and he were one, that the Father was in him and he was in the Father, and that all things belonging to the Father were his. After complete union he said he had power over all flesh (John 17:2) and all power in heaven and on earth (Matthew 28:18). There are also other such passages. The reason why the Lord experienced these two states, the state of being emptied out and the state of being glorified, is that no other method of achieving union could possibly exist. Only this method follows the divine design, and the divine design cannot be changed. The divine design is that we arrange ourselves for receiving God and prepare ourselves as a vessel and a dwelling place where God can enter and live as if we were his own temple. We have to do this preparation by ourselves, yet we have to acknowledge that the preparation comes from God.

This acknowledgment is needed because we do not feel the presence or the actions of God, even though God is in fact intimately present and brings about every good love and every true belief we have. This is the divine design we follow, and have to follow, to go from being earthly to being spiritual. The Lord had to go through the same process to make his earthly human manifestation divine. This is why he prayed to the Father. This is why he did the Father's will. This is why he attributed everything he did and said to the Father. This is why he said on the cross, "My God, my God, why have you abandoned me?" [Matthew 27:46; Mark 15:34]. In this state God appears to be absent. After this state comes a second one, the state of being in a partnership with God. In this second state we do basically the same things, but now we do them with God. We no longer need to attribute to God everything good that we intend and do and everything true that we think and say in the same way as we used to, because now this acknowledgment is written on our heart. It is inside everything we do and everything we say. In this same way, the Lord united himself to his Father and the Father united himself to the Lord. In a nutshell, the Lord glorified his human nature (meaning that he made it divine) in the same way that he regenerates us (meaning that he makes us spiritual). (*True Christianity* §§104–5)

Redemption was actually a matter of gaining control of the hells, restructuring the heavens, and by so doing preparing for a new spiritual church. . . . This new redemption began in the year 1757 along with a Last Judgment that happened at that time. The redemption has continued from then until now. The reason is that today is the Second Coming of the Lord. A new church is being instituted that could not have been instituted unless first the hells were brought under control and the heavens were restructured. (*True Christianity* §115)

[The Lord's] Second Coming [is] an event foretold throughout the Book of Revelation and in Matthew 24:3, 30; Mark 13:26; Luke 21:27; and Acts of the Apostles 1:11, as well as other places.... During his First Coming the hells were swollen with idol-worshipers, sorcerers, and falsifiers of the Word. During this Second Coming the hells are swollen with so-called Christians— some who are steeped in materialist philosophy, and others who have falsified the Word by using it to sanction their made-up faith about three divine persons from eternity and about the Lord's suffering as the true redemption. (*True Christianity* §121)

This Second Coming of the Lord Is Not Taking Place in Person but in the Word, Since the Word Is from Him and He Is the Word (*True Christianity* §§776–78)

Now, however, Christianity itself is arising for the first time. The Lord is now establishing the new church that is meant by the New Jerusalem in the Book of Revelation. In it, God the Father, the Son, and the Holy Spirit are acknowledged as one, because they are together in one person. Therefore the Lord is pleased to reveal the spiritual sense of the Word. (*True Christianity* §700)

This Second Coming of the Lord Is Taking Place by Means of Someone to Whom the Lord Has Manifested Himself in Person and Whom He Has Filled with His Spirit So That That Individual Can Present the Teachings of the New Church on

the Lord's Behalf through the Agency of the Word (*True Christianity* §§779–80)

The Lord ... is going to accomplish this through the agency of a human being who can not only accept these teachings intellectually but also publish them in printed form. I testify in truth that the Lord manifested himself to me, his servant, and assigned me to this task; after doing so, he opened the sight of my spirit and brought me into the spiritual world; and he has allowed me to see the heavens and the hells and to have conversations with angels and spirits on a continual basis for many years now. ... Ever since the first day of this calling, I have accepted nothing regarding the teachings of this church from any angel; what I have received has come from the Lord alone while I was reading the Word. (*True Christianity* §779)

Epilogue

THE LAST CENTURY cannot be said to be a religious era. While churches continue to enroll members, the number of nonbelievers increases far more rapidly. While some theologians—a Barth, a Niebuhr, a Pope Paul—gained worldwide acclaim, theological seminaries fall steadily behind secular graduate schools in both the quantity and quality of their student bodies. While fundamentalist sects continue to insist upon a literal interpretation of the Bible, the vast majority of persons within and without the ranks of organized religion doubt the divine origin of biblical teachings and debate the existence of God himself.

The contradiction known as "Christian atheism" receives scholarly attention as the base of a new theology. Christianity seems to be dissolving in a sea of confused skepticism. William Hamilton finds the modern theologian "alienated from the Bible, just as he is alienated from God and the church." [30] Apart from some psalmist poetry, a few clear prophetic calls, and some of the teachings of Jesus, the Bible speaks with many tongues, few of which appeal to the modern intellect. Thomas J. J. Altizer argues that Christianity faces the "most profound crisis" of its existence because "God has died in *our* time, in *our* history, in *our* existence." He concludes that "affirmation of the traditional forms of faith" is a mere escape from the "brute realities of history." [31] In sum, as the same theologian puts it, "On all sides theologians are agreed that we are now in some sense living in a post-Christian age." [32]

Over the centuries, dogmas have grown up that encumber modern Christianity like a host of barnacles on a ship long at sea. Confusions abound over the nature of God the Father, the personality of Jesus, the place of the Holy Ghost, the workings of the Trinity, the possibility of the Virgin Birth, the quality of the good life, the means by which sins are identified and forgiven, the process of death, the form and existence of life in another world. In an earlier time, perhaps nearly three centuries ago, few of the basic questions of life were raised by the average person. However, the intellectual currents of the nineteenth century—Darwinian evolution, Marxian materialism, Freudian psychoanalytic theories—plus the impact of science and technology undermined the basic assumptions of the fundamentalist view of life. Up until 1925, the old theology still found some support. But when William Jennings Bryan suffered the humiliating ridicule administered by Clarence Darrow in the Scopes trial, literalist interpretations of the Bible ceased to have meaning, and organized religion has remained on the defensive ever since.

Swedenborg would not be surprised at the religious trends of the modern era. Many of his adverse judgments on traditional Christianity sound remarkably current. For those interested, he sorts out the polytheistic tangle of orthodox concepts of God, the process by which Christ's human was made divine, the idea that heaven and hell are not places but states, the causal relationship between the spiritual and natural worlds, and the meaning of the Bible in both its exterior and interior messages. Readers will differ in their understanding of what he has to tell them. But few who are genuinely in search of a more meaningful explanation of life will fail to be impressed by the scope and power of this eighteenth-century thinker's attempt to "explore the mysteries of faith." [33]

Appendix

Published Translations Used for Swedenborg Selections

Divine Love and Wisdom. Translated by George F. Dole. West Chester, PA: Swedenborg Foundation, 2010.

Divine Providence. Translated by George F. Dole. West Chester, PA: Swedenborg Foundation, 2010.

Heaven and Hell. Translated by George F. Dole. West Chester, PA: Swedenborg Foundation, 2010.

Last Judgment / Supplements. Translated by George F. Dole and Jonathan S. Rose. West Chester, PA: Swedenborg Foundation, 2018.

Life / Faith. Translated by George F. Dole. West Chester, PA: Swedenborg Foundation, 2014.

The Lord. Translated by George F. Dole. West Chester, PA: Swedenborg Foundation, 2014.

New Jerusalem. Translated by George F. Dole. West Chester, PA: Swedenborg Foundation, 2016.

Other Planets. Translated by George F. Dole and Jonathan S. Rose. West Chester, PA: Swedenborg Foundation, 2018.

Sacred Scripture / White Horse.[34] Translated by George F. Dole. West Chester, PA: Swedenborg Foundation, 2015.

Secrets of Heaven. 4 vols (§§1–3485). Translated by Lisa Hyatt Cooper. West Chester, PA: Swedenborg Foundation, 2008–22.

True Christianity. 2 vols. Translated by Jonathan S. Rose. West Chester, PA: Swedenborg Foundation, 2006–11.

Unpublished Translations
Used for Swedenborg Selections

Draft Invitation to the New Church. Unpublished section translations by Shannah Conroy and Chara Daum. West Chester, PA: Swedenborg Foundation.

Draft of "Sacred Scripture." Unpublished section translations by Shannah Conroy and Chara Daum. West Chester, PA: Swedenborg Foundation.

Draft of "Supplements." Unpublished section translations by Shannah Conroy and Chara Daum. West Chester, PA: Swedenborg Foundation.

Draft on Divine Love. Unpublished section translations by Shannah Conroy and Chara Daum. West Chester, PA: Swedenborg Foundation.

Draft on Divine Wisdom. Unpublished section translations by Shannah Conroy and Chara Daum. West Chester, PA: Swedenborg Foundation.

Marriage Love. Unpublished section translations by George F. Dole, as edited by Brand Erik Odhner. New Century Edition forthcoming. West Chester, PA: Swedenborg Foundation.

Revelation Explained. Unpublished section translations by Shannah Conroy and Chara Daum, unless otherwise indicated. West Chester, PA: Swedenborg Foundation.

Revelation Unveiled. Unpublished section translations by George F. Dole. New Century Edition forthcoming. West Chester, PA: Swedenborg Foundation.

Secrets of Heaven. Unpublished section translations (§§3486+) by Lisa Hyatt Cooper. New Century Editions forthcoming. West Chester, PA: Swedenborg Foundation.

Sketch for "Coda to True Christianity." Unpublished section translations by Shannah Conroy and Chara Daum. West Chester, PA: Swedenborg Foundation.

Sketch for "True Christianity." Unpublished section translations by Shannah Conroy and Chara Daum. West Chester, PA: Swedenborg Foundation.

Sketch on Goodwill. Unpublished section translations by Shannah Conroy, Chara Daum, and Lisa Hyatt Cooper. West Chester, PA: Swedenborg Foundation.

Survey / Soul-Body Interaction. Unpublished section translations by Jonathan S. Rose and George F. Dole. New Century Edition forthcoming. West Chester, PA: Swedenborg Foundation.

Additional Sources

ALTIZER, Thomas J. J., and William Hamilton. *Radical Theology and the Death of God*. Indianapolis, IN: The Bobbs-Merrill Company, Inc., 1966.

BARRETT, B. F. *The Swedenborg Library*. 12 vols. Germantown, PA: Swedenborg Publishing Association, 1875–81.

BLOCK, Marguerite Beck. *New Church in the New World*. New York: Holt, 1932.

DOYLE, Arthur Conan. *History of Spiritualism*. New York: Doubleday, 1926.

EMERSON, R. W. *Representative Men*. Boston: Houghton Mifflin Co., 1903.

HYDE, James. *Bibliography of the Works of Emanuel Swedenborg*. London: Swedenborg Society, 1906.

JAMES, Henry, Sr. *Christianity the Logic of Creation*. New York: D. Appleton & Co., 1857.

———. *Society the Redeemed Form of Man*. Boston: Houghton Mifflin Co., 1879.

———. *Substance and Shadow*. Boston: Ticknor and Fields, 1866.

KELLER, Helen. *My Religion*. New York: Twayne Publishers, 1968.

PERRY, Bliss, ed. *The Heart of Emerson's Journals*. Boston: Houghton Mifflin Co., 1926.

POTTS, John Faulkner. *Swedenborg Concordance*. 5 vols. London: Swedenborg Society, 1888; 1948.

SEARLE, Arthur H. *General Index to Swedenborg's Scripture Quotations*. London: Swedenborg Society, 1954.

SIGSTEDT, Cyriel O. *The Swedenborg Epic*. New York: Bookman, 1952.

SIMPSON, George Gaylord, and William S. Beck. *Life: An Introduction to Biology*. New York: Harcourt, 1965.

SWEDENBORG, Emanuel. *The Animal Kingdom*. 2 vols. London: Swedenborg Scientific Association, 1960.

TAFEL, R. L. *Documents Concerning the Life and Character of Emanuel Swedenborg*. 2 vols. London: Swedenborg Society, 1875–77.

TOKSVIG, Signe. *Emanuel Swedenborg: Scientist and Mystic*. New Haven: Yale University Press, 1948.

Transactions of the International Swedenborg Congress. London: Swedenborg Society, 1912.

TROBRIDGE, George. *A Life of Swedenborg*. London: Warne & Co., 1912.

WARREN, Samuel M. *A Compendium of the Theological Writings of Emanuel Swedenborg*. London: Swedenborg Society, 1875–1954.

BIBLIOGRAPHICAL NOTE

The Swedenborg Epic by Cyriel O. Sigstedt supplies the best biographical survey. Written from a pro-Swedenborg perspective, it is nevertheless scholarly, comprehensive, and readable. *Emanuel Swedenborg: Scientist and Mystic* by Signe Toksvig provides consistently critical insights by a scholarly skeptic. *A Life of Swedenborg* by George Trobridge, while older and less scholarly, has enjoyed wider circulation than either Sigstedt's or Toksvig's biographies and still gives a relatively accurate overview of Swedenborg's life and works.

R. L. Tafel's *Documents Concerning the Life and Character of Emanuel Swedenborg* brings together a wide variety of primary source material both by and about Swedenborg. Few of these documents have been published elsewhere and, in any case, most of the originals are in Latin or Swedish.

No comprehensive history of the various Swedenborgian sects has been written, but Marguerite Beck Block's *New Church in the New World* provides a perceptive summary of major portions of the New Church story. Probably two-thirds of Swedenborg's followers have been residents of the Western hemisphere.

John Faulkner Potts created an indispensable tool for Swedenborg scholarship during a lifetime of effort in support of Swedenborg studies. His five-volume *Swedenborg Concordance* makes it possible to approach the thirty-volume corpus of Swedenborg's theology from a variety of subject headings. Without this *Concordance,* an almost unlimited amount of time would be required to survey even a few of Swedenborg's teachings.

The comprehensive *Bibliography of the Works of Emanuel Swedenborg* by James Hyde is also useful, as is Arthur H. Searle's *General Index to Swedenborg's Scripture Quotations*.

Samuel M. Warren prepared the best of many previous Swedenborg studies under the title *A Compendium of the Theological Writings of Emanuel Swedenborg*. Those who find the volume in hand interesting may want to consult Warren for further insights. B. F. Barrett's twelve brief volumes of *The Swedenborg Library* illustrate Swedenborg's teachings under major subject headings and employ felicitous translations. The editing and comment are particularly effective, but, unfortunately, the volumes have long been out of print. Warren's, Barrett's, and virtually every one of the some twenty other Swedenborgian compendiums were prepared essentially for use by persons already familiar with Swedenborg's writings. Hopefully, this new study will have a wider appeal.

ENDNOTES

1. Swedenborg's writings and various collateral materials are distributed by the Swedenborg Foundation, 320 North Church Street, West Chester, PA 19380. A list of Swedenborg's theological writings can be found at swedenborg.com/emanuel-swedenborg/writings/.

2. R. W. Emerson, *Representative Men* (Boston: Houghton Miffin Co., 1903), 102, 103.

3. Henry James, Sr., *Christianity the Logic of Creation* (New York: D. Appleton & Co., 1857), 81, and *Substance and Shadow* (Boston: Ticknor and Fields, 1866), 104. James also wrote, "If intellectual power is to be measured by the measure of truth possessed, it would seem unaffectedly ludicrous, to any one acquainted with his writings, that any other person in the intellectual history of the race should 'be named' . . . 'in the same day with him'" (*Society the Redeemed Form of Man* [Boston: Houghton Mifflin Co., 1879], 138).

4. Edwin Markham, "Swedenborg, a Colossus in the World of Thought," *The New York American,* October 7, 1911. See also Markham's handwritten note in the flyleaf of his copy of Swedenborg's *Heaven and Hell,* Markham Collection, Wagner College Library, Staten Island.

5. Helen Keller, *My Religion* (New York: Twayne Publishers, 1968), 17, 27, 28, 33.

6. See "Tenth Letter of Emanuel Swedenborg to Dr. Beyer," in R. L. Tafel, *Documents Concerning the Life and Character of Emanuel Swedenborg* (London: Swedenborg Society, 1875–77), vol. II, 279.

7. Swedenborg was only eleven years old, but entering upon university work at such an age was not unusual for the time.

8. Cyriel O. Sigstedt, *The Swedenborg Epic* (New York: Bookman, 1952), 11.

9. See "Memorial to the Houses of the Diet by Em. Swedenborg," in Tafel, *Documents,* vol. I, 512.

10. George Gaylord Simpson and William S. Beck, *Life: An Introduction to Biology* (New York: Harcourt, 1965), 827–28.

11. In 1910, in celebration of its 100th anniversary, and the 200th anniversary of Swedenborg's first trip to London, England, the Swedenborg Society of London sponsored an International Swedenborg Congress. King Gustav V of Sweden was the honorary patron, and delegates came from all over the world. Swedenborg's contributions in science, philosophy, and theology were treated in more than forty scholarly papers by a

variety of learned persons. The scientific papers were delivered by some eminent twentieth-century scholars. See *Transactions of the International Swedenborg Congress* (London: Swedenborg Society, 1912).

12. O. M. Ramström, "Swedenborg on the Cerebral Cortex as the Seat of Psychical Activity," in *Transactions of the International Swedenborg Congress*, 56.

13. Sigstedt, *Swedenborg Epic*, 116–17, 454n170, 472n569.

14. Emanuel Swedenborg, *The Animal Kingdom* (London: Swedenborg Scientific Association, 1960), vol. I, 15.

15. See "Robsahm's Memoirs of Swedenborg," in Tafel, *Documents*, vol. I, 35–36 (Swedenborg's account as related to Carl Robsahm, a Stockholm banker and friend of the Swedenborg family).

16. The individual theological works by Swedenborg are listed in the appendix to this study.

17. The many similar accounts of this incident and the two succeeding ones are synthesized and cited in Sigstedt, *Swedenborg Epic*, 269–82.

18. See "Testimony of the Rev. Arvid Ferelius," in Tafel, *Documents*, vol. II, 560.

19. The best account of the Gothenburg heresy trial is found in Sigstedt, *Swedenborg Epic*, 387–409.

20. See "Robsahm's Memoirs of Swedenborg," in Tafel, *Documents*, vol. I, 38–39.

21. Johann Christian Cuno, as quoted in Sigstedt, *Swedenborg Epic*, 415.

22. Tafel, *Documents*, vol. II, 564–65 (from "John Wesley's Testimony Concerning Swedenborg in 1772, and 1773"), 546 (from "Testimony Collected by Henry Peckitt, Esq.").

23. Tafel, *Documents*, vol. II, 580 (from "The Charge of Swedenborg Having Retracted His Writings in His Last Moments Critically Examined"), 557–58 (from "Testimony of the Rev. Arvid Ferelius").

24. Tafel, *Documents*, vol. II, 578, 568–69.

25. Arthur Conan Doyle, *History of Spiritualism* (New York: Doubleday, 1926), 22.

26. All number references in the text refer to sections ($), not pages, in conformity with Swedenborg's own numbering system.

27. Swedenborg consistently uses "the Word" to refer to a somewhat shortened version of the Bible. In his view, the Word of God was given to humanity in the Bible, except for only certain books that do not contain divine teachings throughout.

28. Swedenborg's use of the spelling "conjugial" as preferred to the more common spelling "conjugal" is consistent throughout his theological writings. Doubtless he sought to underscore his belief in the distinctive quality of his teachings on marriage love.

29. Bliss Perry, ed., *The Heart of Emerson's Journals* (Boston: Houghton Mifflin Co., 1926), 48.

30. William Hamilton, "Thursday's Child," in Thomas J. J. Altizer and William Hamilton, *Radical Theology and the Death of God* (Indianapolis, IN: The Bobbs-Merrill Company, Inc., 1966), 90.

31. Thomas J. J. Altizer, "Theology and the Death of God," in Altizer and Hamilton, *Radical Theology and the Death of God*, 95.

32. Thomas J. J. Altizer, "America and the Future of Theology," in Altizer and Hamilton, *Radical Theology and the Death of God*, 9.

33. Emanuel Swedenborg, *True Christianity* (West Chester, PA: Swedenborg Foundation, 2011), vol. II, §508.

34. *White Horse* deals largely with the subject of divine revelation and humanity's need for it. Its title comes from Revelation 19 (the internal sense of which is discussed): "Then I saw heaven opened, and there was a white horse! Its rider is called Faithful and True, and in righteousness he judges and makes war. His eyes are like a flame of fire, and on his head are many diadems; and he has a name inscribed that no one knows but himself. He is clothed in a robe dipped in blood, and his name is called The Word of God. And the armies of heaven, wearing fine linen, white and pure, were following him on white horses. From his mouth comes a sharp sword with which to strike down the nations, and he will rule them with a rod of iron; he will tread the wine press of the fury of the wrath of God the Almighty. On his robe and on his thigh he has a name inscribed, 'King of kings and Lord of lords'" (Revelation 19:11–16 [NRSV]).

Index